A *Campbell* COOKBOOK

COOKING
WITH
SOUP

Recipes developed and tested by Home Economists of Campbell Kitchens
Campbell Soup Company, Camden, N. J.

Thirteenth printing—revised March, 1976
Over 4,800,000 copies in print

Table of Contents

Introduction . . .

Of all the convenience foods that give you a head start to better meals, soups are probably the most versatile.

When you open a can of soup—to use as soup, or as a sauce, or as a cooking ingredient—you have much of the work already done for you.

A casserole is half ready at the start when soup is the sauce—as are many other meat and vegetable dishes. Serve a bowl of soup and you have a meal well on the way. Just open a can of any of the following kinds for appealing eating and easier cooking.

Here are more than 50 kinds for your selection.

CONDENSED SOUPS

Asparagus, Cream of
Bean with Bacon
Beef
Beef Broth (Bouillon)
Beef Noodle
Black Bean
Celery, Cream of
Cheddar Cheese
Chicken Broth
Chicken, Cream of
Chicken 'n Dumplings
Chicken Gumbo
Chicken Noodle
Chicken Noodle-O's
Chicken with Rice
Chicken & Stars
Chicken Vegetable
Chili Beef
Clam Chowder (Manhattan Style)
Clam Chowder, New England
Consommé (beef, gelatin added)
Curly Noodle
Golden Vegetable Noodle-O's
Green Pea

Hot Dog Bean
Minestrone
Mushroom, Cream of
Mushroom, Golden
Noodles & Ground Beef
Onion
Onion, Cream of
Oyster Stew
Pepper Pot
Potato, Cream of
Scotch Broth
Shrimp, Cream of
Split Pea with Ham
Stockpot
Tomato
Tomato-Beef Noodle-O's
Tomato, Bisque
Tomato Rice
Turkey Noodle
Turkey Vegetable
Vegetable
Vegetable, Old Fashioned
Vegetable Beef
Vegetarian Vegetable

READY TO SERVE SOUPS

CHUNKY SOUPS
Chunky Beef
Chunky Chicken
Chunky Chicken with Rice
Chunky Clam Chowder
Chunky Sirloin Burger
Chunky Split Pea with Ham
Chunky Turkey
Chunky Vegetable

LOW SODIUM SOUPS
Green Pea
Mushroom, Cream of
Tomato
Turkey Noodle
Vegetable
Vegetable Beef

Meeting Nutritional Needs

Nutrition is what you eat and how your body uses it. It is your total daily food intake transformed into physical appearance, energy, growth, and countless other body functions.

Happily, your nutrition is in your own hands. Your decisions really count when it comes to the food you eat. Whether you buy and prepare food to be eaten at home or you eat out, you are faced with important food choices. How can you be sure that what you are choosing is the best?

After all, each of us has different nutritional needs, and these needs are constantly changing. Children's needs are dictated by their growth patterns. Adult needs change with age. One set of rules simply cannot apply to everyone. And yet, there is a practical guide to good nutrition: The Four Food Groups. It translates the technical knowledge of nutrition into a simple plan for everyday eating, providing sound advice on the kind and quantity of food necessary to meet your body's needs.

FOUR FOOD GROUPS
YOU SHOULD EAT A VARIETY OF FOODS
FROM EACH GROUP EVERY DAY. (Note: EVERY DAY)

Milk Group

Items in this group are a primary source of calcium. They also provide protein, riboflavin, vitamin A, and vitamin D.

2 to 3 cups of milk—children under 9
3 or more cups   —children 9 to 12
4 or more cups   —teenagers
2 or more cups   —adults

This can be whole or skim milk, evaporated or dry milk, or buttermilk.

Common portions of various kinds of cheese and ice cream and their milk equivalents are:

1-inch cube Cheddar-type cheese=½ cup milk
½ cup cottage cheese   =⅓ cup milk
2 tablespoons cream cheese   =1 tablespoon milk
½ cup ice cream   =¼ cup milk

Vegetable-Fruit Group

Items in this group are counted on to supply most of the ascorbic acid (vitamin C), as well as much of the vitamin A, some iron and other minerals.

4 or more servings every day including:

1 serving of citrus fruit or juice, or tomato
1 serving of dark green or deep yellow vegetable
2 or more servings of other vegetables and fruit, including potatoes.

One serving is ½ cup of vegetable or fruit or a portion as ordinarily served, such as one medium banana, etc.

Meat Group

Items in this group supply protein, iron, thiamine, riboflavin, and niacin.

2 or more servings of beef, lamb, liver, pork, veal, poultry, fish, or eggs.

One serving is 2 to 3 ounces of lean cooked meat, poultry or fish, all without bone; two eggs. One cup cooked dry beans, peas, lentils; 4 tablespoons peanut butter; nuts; and cereal with milk contribute to the meat group.

Bread-Cereal Group

Items in this group supply many of the vitamins in the B group, iron, and carbohydrate.

4 servings or more of enriched or whole-grain breads and cereals. This group also includes enriched flour, macaroni and spaghetti, noodles, rice and rolled oats, etc.

One serving is 1 slice of bread, 1 ounce ready-to-eat cereal, ½ to ¾ cup cooked cereal, cornmeal, macaroni, rice, grits, noodles, or spaghetti.

To round out meals, experts urge us to include foods not included within the Groups. These might include butter, margarine, sugars . . . many of which are often found in everyday meal patterns or as ingredients in recipes. Some vegetable oil can also be included among the fats used.

For soups that contribute to the Four Food Groups see page 130.

Suggestions for Cooking with Condensed Soups

A can of condensed soup is a constant help in your kitchen—whether you use it for white sauce in a casserole or for cooking liquid in a stew.

The cream soups, which are useful in so many recipes, include:

Cream of Celery   Cream of Mushroom
Cream of Chicken

Often one kind of cream soup may be substituted for another. You will find recipes suggesting this all through the book.

Other soups with countless uses are:

Cheddar Cheese   Golden Mushroom   Tomato

The following chart gives you some "rules of thumb" to use in creating your own recipes with condensed soups as cooking sauces (see SAUCERY chapter for special sauces with specific directions):

Tomato Souper Sauce   Use condensed tomato soup just as it comes from the can or thin a bit with water, if desired. Season as you like with a little prepared mustard, horse-radish, herbs, Worcestershire, etc. Use as pour-on sauce for hamburgers, pork chops, and other meats.

Gravy	Add a can of condensed cream soup or golden mushroom soup to 2 to 3 tablespoons of meat drippings (or butter); stir in water or milk for thickness desired.
White Sauce or Cream Sauce	Use canned condensed cream soups or Cheddar cheese soup in almost any recipe that calls for white sauce or cream sauce. Thin with ¼ cup milk or water for medium white sauce for dishes such as creamed chicken or creamed vegetables. One can makes enough sauce for 1 to 1½ cups diced or chopped cooked meat (chicken, turkey, ham, tuna, shrimp, crab) or 4 sliced hard-cooked eggs . . . plus seasonings as desired. One can soup also makes enough pour-on sauce for: 1 pound meat as meat loaf, 1 pound fish fillets, 2 pounds chicken parts, 2 cups cooked vegetables (two 1-pound cans; two 10-ounce packages, frozen), 6 chops, 4 to 6 sandwiches.
Casseroles	1 can of any condensed cream soup (or Cheddar cheese or tomato soup) plus ¼ cup water or milk (or more as needed) makes enough sauce for about 2 cups cooked macaroni or noodles (about 4 ounces uncooked) or 1½ cups cooked rice (about ½ cup uncooked). Add seasonings and cooked meat or vegetables as desired.
Meat Stock or Broth	Use canned condensed beef broth or chicken broth or consommé in place of homemade stock. Good for many kinds of stews and pot roasts.
Chicken Stew	Use any of the cream soups, chicken broth, or chicken soups for part of liquid for cooking. If using a vegetable soup or one with noodles or rice, add towards end of cooking time.
Meat Stew or Pot Roast	Use consommé, beef broth, chicken broth, golden mushroom or tomato soup for part of liquid to cook meat. For vegetables in stew, use one of vegetable soups; add towards end of cooking time since vegetables are already cooked.
Homemade Soup	Add canned condensed soup for flavor and body.

Note about using this book: Asterisks (*) are used in menus to show items for which there are recipes. Recipes are listed in index at end of book.

Skillet And Top-Stove Dishes

These dishes cook in one pan—and quickly. Homemakers love their easygoing versatility. Everyone loves their taste. Who could ask for more?

The basics of skillet-cooking are simple:

Choose a heavy-bottomed pan that heats evenly and is roomy enough to hold all ingredients without crowding. Many recipes may also be prepared in a chafing dish, large heavy saucepan, or electric skillet.

Combine several foods. As in casseroles, most stove-top recipes call for meat, fish, or cheese—plus pasta, rice, or potatoes—plus sauce.

When the sauce is a condensed soup, the eating is superlative. Condensed soups impart extra flavor while uniting the remaining ingredients.

Serve your speedy supper dish piping hot with crisp salad and warm rolls. Now—collect the compliments.

SALISBURY STEAK

1 can (10¾ ounces) condensed
   golden mushroom soup
1½ pounds ground beef
½ cup fine dry bread crumbs
¼ cup finely chopped onion
1 egg, slightly beaten
⅓ cup water

Mix thoroughly ¼ cup soup, beef, bread crumbs, onion, and egg; shape into 6 patties. In skillet, brown patties (use shortening if necessary); pour off fat. Blend in remaining soup and water. Cover; cook over low heat 20 minutes or until done. Stir occasionally. Makes 6 servings.

MACARONI AND CHEESE

¼ cup chopped onion
1 tablespoon butter or margarine
1 can (10¾ ounces) condensed
   cream of mushroom soup
½ cup milk
3 cups cooked elbow macaroni
1½ cups shredded Cheddar cheese

In saucepan, cook onion in butter until tender. Blend in soup and milk; add macaroni and cheese. Heat until cheese melts; stir occasionally. Makes about 4 cups.

BEEF MEXICALI

3½-pound boneless chuck roast,
   well-trimmed
2 tablespoons flour
2 tablespoons shortening
1 can (16 ounces) tomatoes
½ cup water
1 cup chopped onion
2 teaspoons chili powder
1 can (11¼ ounces) condensed
   chili beef soup
½ cup diced green pepper
Corn bread or cooked rice

Cut meat into thin strips; sprinkle with flour. In skillet, brown meat in shortening; pour off fat. Add tomatoes, water, onion, and chili powder. Cover; cook over low heat 1 hour. Add soup and green pepper; cook covered ½ hour more or until tender. Stir occasionally. Serve over bread. Makes about 6½ cups.

PORCUPINE MEATBALLS
(pictured on cover)

1 can (10¾ ounces) condensed
   tomato soup
1 pound ground beef
1 cup quick-cooking rice, uncooked
1 egg, slightly beaten
¼ cup finely chopped onion
1 teaspoon salt
Generous dash pepper
¾ cup water
1 teaspoon prepared mustard
1 small clove garlic, minced

Mix thoroughly ¼ cup soup, beef, rice, egg, onion, salt, and pepper. Shape *firmly* into 16 meatballs. In skillet, brown meatballs (use shortening if necessary); pour off fat. Blend in remaining soup, water, mustard, and garlic. Cover; cook over low heat 20 minutes or until done. Stir occasionally. Makes about 4 cups.

CHICKEN HASH

1 can (10¾ ounces) condensed
 cream of mushroom soup
⅓ cup milk
1 can (5 ounces) boned chicken or
 turkey, or 1 cup diced cooked
 chicken or turkey
1 can (8 ounces) cut green beans,
 drained
2 tablespoons diced pimiento
Dash nutmeg
Dash pepper
3 cups hot cooked rice

In saucepan, blend soup and milk;
add chicken, beans, pimiento, nutmeg, and pepper. Heat slowly; stir
often. Serve over cooked rice.
Makes about 4 cups.

SOUPER LEFTOVERS

1½ cups cubed roast, steak,
 or chicken
1 cup leftover vegetables
1 can (10¾ ounces) condensed
 cream of celery soup
Milk or water as needed
Toast

In saucepan, combine all ingredients
except toast. Heat; stir occasionally.
Serve over toast or in patty shells.
Makes about 2½ cups.
VARIATIONS: Substitute cream of
chicken, mushroom, or tomato soup
for cream of celery soup.

HE-MAN SPANISH RICE

1 pound ground beef
½ cup chopped green pepper
½ cup chopped onion
1 large clove garlic, minced
1 can (10¾ ounces) condensed
 tomato soup
1½ cups water
1½ cups quick-cooking rice,
 uncooked
1 tablespoon Worcestershire
½ teaspoon salt
Generous dash pepper

In skillet, cook beef, green pepper,
and onion with garlic until vegetables are tender; stir to separate
meat. Add remaining ingredients.
Cover; cook over low heat 10 minutes or until liquid is absorbed. Stir
occasionally. Makes about 5 cups.

VEAL PARMESAN

1 pound thinly sliced veal cutlet
Salt
Pepper
1 egg, slightly beaten
1 tablespoon water
½ cup fine dry bread crumbs
3 tablespoons shortening
1 can (10¾ ounces) condensed
tomato soup
¼ cup water
¼ cup finely chopped onion
1 small clove garlic, minced
Dash ground thyme
4 slices (about 4 ounces)
Mozzarella cheese
¼ cup grated Parmesan cheese

Pound veal; season with salt and pepper. Cut into serving-size pieces. Beat egg and 1 tablespoon water. Dip veal in egg mixture, then in bread crumbs. In skillet, brown veal in shortening (use additional shortening if necessary). Arrange veal in 2-quart shallow baking dish (12x8 x2"). Mix soup, ¼ cup water, onion, garlic, and thyme; pour over veal. Top with Mozzarella and Parmesan cheese. Bake at 350°F. for 20 minutes or until veal is tender. Makes 4 servings.

SKILLET FRANKS 'N NOODLES

1 pound frankfurters, cut in half
diagonally
½ cup chopped onion
½ teaspoon basil or oregano leaves,
crushed
2 tablespoons butter or margarine
1 can (10¾ ounces) condensed
cream of celery or mushroom soup
½ cup milk
½ cup chopped canned tomatoes
2 cups cooked wide noodles
2 tablespoons chopped parsley

In skillet, brown frankfurters and cook onion with basil in butter until tender. Stir in remaining ingredients. Heat; stir occasionally. Makes about 4 cups.

CHOP SOUPY

1 pound round steak (½" thick)
1½ cups diagonally sliced celery
1 medium green pepper, cut in
1-inch squares
2 tablespoons salad oil
1 can (10¾ ounces) condensed
golden mushroom soup
⅓ cup water
1 tablespoon soy sauce
½ cup green onions sliced
diagonally in 1-inch pieces
Cooked rice

Freeze meat 1 hour to firm (makes slicing easier); slice into *very* thin strips. In skillet, cook celery and green pepper in oil until *just* tender; push to one side. Add meat; cook until color changes (about 3 to 4 minutes). Add soup, water, soy, and green onions. Heat; stir occasionally. Serve over rice. Makes about 4½ cups.

SPAGHETTI SOUTHERN STYLE

2 slices bacon
1 medium onion, chopped
1½ teaspoons chili powder
1 large clove garlic, minced
1 can (10¾ ounces) condensed
  tomato soup
½ cup water
1 cup diced cooked beef
1 medium green pepper,
  cut in strips
Cooked spaghetti

In saucepan, cook bacon until crisp; remove and crumble. Cook onion with chili powder and garlic in drippings until tender. Stir in soup, water, beef, and green pepper. Cover; cook over low heat 30 minutes. Stir occasionally. Serve over spaghetti. Garnish with bacon. Makes about 2½ cups.

SPAGHETTI FRANKFURTER SUPPER

½ cup chopped celery
½ cup chopped onion
2 tablespoons shortening
1 pound frankfurters, cut in
  ½-inch slices
1 can (10¾ ounces) condensed
  tomato soup
½ cup water
1 teaspoon Worcestershire
Cooked spaghetti

Cook celery and onion in shortening until tender. Add frankfurters; cook until lightly browned. Stir in soup, water, and Worcestershire. Cook about 15 minutes to blend flavors; stir often. Serve over hot cooked spaghetti. Makes about 3 cups.

TUNA SHORTCAKE

1 can (10¾ ounces) condensed
  cream of celery, chicken, or
  mushroom soup
¼ cup milk
1 can (about 7 ounces) tuna,
  drained and flaked
1 cup cooked peas
1 tablespoon chopped pimiento
Hot biscuits or toast

Blend soup and milk; add tuna, peas, and pimiento. Heat; stir often. Serve over biscuits or toast. Makes about 2½ cups.

SKILLET CHICKEN DELIGHT

2 pounds chicken parts
¼ cup flour
¼ cup shortening
1 can (10¾ ounces) condensed
  chicken gumbo soup
2 tablespoons ketchup

Dust chicken with flour. In skillet, brown chicken in shortening; pour off fat. Stir in soup and ketchup. Cover; cook over low heat 45 minutes or until tender. Stir occasionally. Makes 4 servings.

TUNA A LA KING

½ cup sliced celery
2 tablespoons chopped onion
1 tablespoon butter or margarine
1 can (10¾ ounces) condensed
   cream of mushroom soup
⅓ cup milk
1 can (about 7 ounces) tuna,
   drained and flaked
2 tablespoons chopped pimiento
Chopped parsley
Toast or biscuits

In saucepan, cook celery and onion in butter until tender. Blend in soup; gradually stir in milk. Add tuna and pimiento. Heat; stir occasionally. Garnish with parsley. Serve over toast. Makes about 2½ cups.

LAST MINUTE SUPPER

1 can (12 ounces) luncheon meat,
   cut in strips
1 medium onion, thinly sliced
2 tablespoons butter or margarine
1 can (10¾ ounces) condensed
   cream of mushroom soup
½ cup milk
2 cups cubed cooked potatoes
2 tablespoons chopped parsley
Dash pepper

In skillet, brown meat and cook onion in butter until tender. Blend in soup and milk. Add remaining ingredients. Heat; stir occasionally. Makes about 5½ cups.

TUNA BEAN SUPPER DISH

⅓ cup chopped onion
2 tablespoons butter or margarine
1 can (10¾ ounces) condensed
   chicken broth
1½ cups quick-cooking rice,
   uncooked
¼ cup sliced water chestnuts
1 teaspoon soy sauce
1 can (about 7 ounces) tuna,
   drained and flaked
1 cup cooked Italian green beans

In saucepan, cook onion in butter until tender. Add broth, rice, water chestnuts, and soy. Bring to a boil; stir. Reduce heat. Cover; cook over low heat 5 minutes or until rice is done and all liquid is absorbed. Add tuna and beans. Heat; stir occasionally. Serve with additional soy. Makes about 4 cups.

Casseroles to Your Credit

Hail to the casserole—wonderful way to bring a tasty meal to the table right in its baking dish.

Choose your own reason for making a casserole tonight. You probably have the ingredients on hand—some meat, fish, poultry, or cheese plus pasta, rice, or potatoes to extend them. A vegetable adds contrasting color and texture.

Now for the perfect sauce that's ready at your fingertips—a can of soup. It seasons and brings together all the other ingredients. The cream soups—cream of celery, mushroom, chicken—and Cheddar cheese soup blend beautifully with almost any casserole combination. Tomato soup also wins honors. And remember—one soup may often be substituted for another with delightful results.

Prepare casseroles in advance if you wish and refrigerate or freeze before baking. Either way, allow extra baking time. Another advantage—casseroles wait patiently in a low oven when dinner is delayed. Children eating ahead? Just prepare several smaller baking dishes.

Feeding unexpected company is a breeze—reach for a can of soup and the ingredients in the following recipes. Another good casserole on the way!

PERFECT TUNA

1 can (10¾ ounces) condensed cream of celery, chicken, or mushroom soup
¼ cup milk
2 cans (about 7 ounces each) tuna, drained and flaked
2 hard-cooked eggs, sliced
1 cup cooked peas
1 cup slightly crumbled potato chips

In 1-quart casserole, blend soup and milk; stir in tuna, eggs, and peas. Bake at 350°F. for 25 minutes or until hot; stir. Top with chips; bake 5 minutes more. Makes about 4 cups.

TOMATO BEEF CASSEROLE

1 pound ground beef
½ cup chopped onion
1 cup shredded Cheddar cheese
1 can (10¾ ounces) condensed
  tomato soup
2 cups cooked medium noodles
1 cup cooked corn
¼ cup water
½ teaspoon salt

In saucepan, brown beef and cook onion until tender; stir to separate meat. Pour off fat. Stir in ¾ cup cheese and remaining ingredients. Pour into 1½-quart casserole. Bake at 350°F. for 30 minutes or until hot; stir. Top with remaining cheese. Makes about 5 cups.

YANKEE NOODLE BAKE

½ pound frankfurters, cut in
  ½-inch pieces
¼ cup chopped onion
2 tablespoons butter or margarine
1 can (10¾ ounces) condensed
  tomato soup
⅓ cup water
1 teaspoon prepared mustard
2 cups cooked noodles
2 tablespoons buttered bread
  crumbs

In saucepan, brown frankfurters and cook onion in butter until tender. Stir in remaining ingredients except crumbs. Pour into 1-quart casserole. Bake at 350°F. for 25 minutes or until hot; stir. Top with crumbs. Bake 5 minutes more. Makes about 3½ cups.

CHICKEN PIE

1½ cups cubed cooked chicken
1 cup cubed cooked potatoes
1 cup cooked mixed vegetables
1 can (10¾ ounces) condensed
  cream of chicken soup
½ cup milk
1 tablespoon finely chopped onion
Generous dash poultry seasoning
1 cup biscuit mix
¼ cup cold water

In 1½-quart casserole, combine all ingredients except biscuit mix and water. Bake at 450°F. for 15 minutes; stir. Meanwhile, combine biscuit mix and water as directed on package; spoon 6 biscuits around edge of casserole. Bake 15 minutes more or until biscuits are done. Makes about 4 cups.

SAVORY SPAGHETTI CASSEROLE

1 pound ground beef
½ cup chopped onion
¼ cup chopped green pepper
1 medium clove garlic, minced
1 can (10¾ ounces) condensed cream of mushroom soup
1 can (10¾ ounces) condensed tomato soup
1 cup water
1 cup shredded sharp process cheese
4 cups cooked spaghetti

In skillet, brown meat and cook onion and green pepper with garlic until tender (use shortening if necessary). Stir to separate meat. Add soups, water, ½ cup cheese, and spaghetti. Pour into 2-quart casserole. Bake at 350°F. for 30 minutes or until hot; stir. Top with remaining cheese. Bake until cheese melts. Makes about 7½ cups.

TURKEY STROGANOFF

¼ cup diced green pepper
¼ cup chopped onion
2 tablespoons butter or margarine
1 can (10¾ ounces) condensed cream of mushroom soup
½ cup sour cream
2 cups cooked noodles
1½ cups cubed cooked turkey
½ teaspoon paprika

In saucepan, cook green pepper and onion in butter until tender. In 1½-quart casserole, blend soup and sour cream. Stir in remaining ingredients. Bake at 350°F. for 35 minutes or until hot; stir. Sprinkle with additional paprika. Makes about 4½ cups.

CAPTAIN'S CHOICE

½ cup sliced celery
2 tablespoons chopped onion
2 tablespoons butter or margarine
1 can (10¾ ounces) condensed cream of mushroom soup
⅓ cup milk
1½ cups diced cooked shrimp
1 cup cooked peas
Dash ground thyme
2 cups seasoned mashed potatoes
¼ cup shredded process cheese

In saucepan, cook celery and onion in butter until tender. Blend in soup, milk, shrimp, peas, and thyme. Pour into 2-quart casserole; spoon potatoes around edge of casserole. Bake at 400°F. for 25 minutes or until hot. Sprinkle with cheese. Bake until cheese melts. Makes about 3½ cups.

16

FIX AHEAD CHICKEN

(pictured on cover)

2 pounds chicken parts
2 tablespoons shortening
1 can (10¾ ounces) condensed
    cream of chicken soup
¼ cup milk
8 small whole white onions
    (about ½ pound)
¼ teaspoon poultry seasoning
¼ teaspoon salt
⅛ teaspoon pepper
2 cups carrots cut in ½-inch slices
1 package (10 ounces) frozen
    Fordhook lima beans

In skillet, brown chicken in shortening; pour off fat. Stir in soup, milk, onion, and seasonings. Cover; cook over low heat 15 minutes. Add carrots and beans. Cook 10 minutes more; stir occasionally. Arrange in 10-inch round baking dish; cover. Store in freezer. To reheat: Place covered casserole in cold oven. Bake at 400°F. for 1 hour 15 minutes; uncover. Bake 15 minutes more or until chicken is tender. Makes 4 servings.
Refrigerator Method: Omit freezing. Refrigerate overnight. Bake covered at 400°F. for 45 minutes; uncover. Bake 15 minutes more or until chicken is tender.

TUNA CASSEROLE

1 can (10¾ ounces) condensed
    cream of celery soup
½ cup milk
2 cups cooked noodles
2 tablespoons chopped parsley
2 tablespoons diced pimiento
2 cans (about 7 ounces each) tuna,
    drained and flaked
2 tablespoons buttered bread
    crumbs

In 1½-quart casserole, combine soup and milk; stir in noodles, parsley, pimiento, and tuna. Bake at 400°F. for 25 minutes or until hot; stir. Top with bread crumbs; bake 5 minutes more. Makes about 4½ cups.

AU GRATIN SPINACH AND NOODLES

1 can (10¾ ounces) condensed
    cream of mushroom soup
⅛ teaspoon ground nutmeg
2 packages (10 ounces each)
    frozen chopped spinach,
    cooked and drained
2 cups cooked noodles
½ cup milk
1 cup shredded process cheese

In 1½-quart casserole, combine all ingredients except cheese. Bake at 350°F. for 30 minutes; stir. Top with cheese. Bake until cheese melts. Makes about 5 cups.

FAVORITE HAM 'N POTATO BAKE

1 can (10¾ ounces) condensed
   cream of mushroom soup
½ cup milk
Dash pepper
4 cups thinly sliced potatoes
1½ cups diced cooked ham
1 small onion, thinly sliced
1 tablespoon butter or margarine
Dash paprika

Combine soup, milk, and pepper. In 2-quart casserole, arrange alternate layers of potatoes, ham, onion, and sauce (cover ham completely with sauce). Dot top with butter; sprinkle with paprika. Cover; bake at 375°F. for 1 hour. Uncover; bake 15 minutes more or until potatoes are done. Makes about 4 cups.

MACARONI AND CHEESE—FAMILY STYLE

¼ cup chopped onion
2 tablespoons butter or margarine
1 can (11 ounces) condensed
   Cheddar cheese soup
½ cup milk
1 tablespoon prepared mustard
¼ teaspoon salt
Generous dash pepper
3 cups cooked elbow macaroni
2 tablespoons buttered bread
   crumbs

In saucepan, cook onion in butter until tender; blend in soup. Gradually stir in milk, mustard, salt, and pepper; add macaroni. Pour into 1½-quart casserole. Bake at 400°F. for 25 minutes or until hot; stir. Top with crumbs; bake 5 minutes more. Makes about 4 cups.

OYSTER 'N HAM NOODLE BAKE

1 cup chopped cooked ham
¼ cup chopped onion
2 tablespoons butter or margarine
2 tablespoons flour
1 can (10½ ounces) condensed
   oyster stew
¼ cup milk
Dash hot pepper sauce
1½ cups cooked noodles
Grated Parmesan cheese

In saucepan, brown ham and cook onion in butter until tender. Blend in flour; gradually stir in stew, milk, and hot pepper sauce. Cook, stirring until thickened. In 1-quart casserole, combine soup mixture with noodles. Top with cheese. Bake at 350°F. for 30 minutes or until hot. Makes about 2½ cups.

PORK CHOP-BEAN BAKE

6 pork chops (about 1½ pounds)
1 can (10¾ ounces) condensed
   cream of celery or mushroom soup
1 package (9 ounces) frozen cut
   green beans, partially thawed
Dash crushed thyme leaves
¼ teaspoon salt
⅛ teaspoon pepper

In oven-proof skillet, brown chops; remove from pan. Pour off fat; stir in soup, beans, and thyme. Arrange chops on top; sprinkle with salt and pepper. Cover; bake at 350°F. for 45 minutes or until chops are tender. 4 servings.

CHEESY TUNA BAKE

¼ cup chopped onion
2 tablespoons butter or margarine
1 can (10¾ ounces) condensed
   cream of celery soup
⅓ cup water
1 cup shredded sharp Cheddar
   cheese
2 cups cooked noodles
1 can (about 7 ounces) tuna,
   drained and flaked
2 tablespoons diced pimiento

In saucepan, cook onion in butter until tender. Stir in soup, water, ¾ cup cheese, noodles, tuna, and pimiento. Pour into 1-quart casserole. Bake at 350°F. for 25 minutes or until hot; stir. Top with remaining cheese. Bake until cheese melts. Makes about 4 cups.

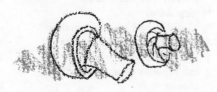

CHICK 'N HAM BAKE

1 can (4 ounces) sliced mushrooms, drained
2 tablespoons chopped onion
2 tablespoons chopped green pepper
1 small clove garlic, minced
Dash crushed thyme leaves
2 tablespoons butter or margarine
1 can (10¾ ounces) condensed cream of chicken soup
2 cups cooked spaghetti
1½ cups diced cooked ham
1 cup chopped canned tomatoes

In saucepan, brown mushrooms and cook onion and green pepper with garlic and thyme in butter until tender. Add remaining ingredients; pour into 1½-quart casserole. Bake at 400°F. for 25 minutes or until hot; stir. Makes about 5 cups.

OVEN MACARONI

1 can (11 ounces) condensed tomato bisque soup
⅓ cup water
1½ cups shredded Cheddar cheese
2 tablespoons grated Parmesan cheese
1 teaspoon oregano leaves, crushed
⅛ teaspoon garlic salt
2 cups cooked spiral-shaped macaroni

In 1-quart casserole, blend soup, water, cheeses, and seasoning. Stir in macaroni. Bake at 400°F. for 25 minutes or until hot; stir. Garnish with green pepper rings if desired. Makes about 3½ cups.

PINWHEEL CASSEROLE

1½ cups cubed cooked beef, lamb, pork, or veal
¼ teaspoon oregano leaves, crushed
2 tablespoons butter or margarine
1 can (10¾ ounces) condensed golden mushroom soup
½ cup water
½ cup chopped canned tomatoes
1 cup cooked cut green beans
1 cup biscuit mix
2 tablespoons grated Parmesan cheese

In saucepan, brown meat with oregano in butter. Stir in soup, ¼ cup water, tomatoes, and green beans. Pour into 1½-quart casserole. Bake at 450°F. for 10 minutes. Meanwhile, combine biscuit mix and ¼ cup cold water; mix as directed on package. Roll out into 8-inch square; sprinkle with cheese. Roll up jelly roll fashion; cut into 8 slices. Place biscuits around edge. Bake 15 minutes more or until browned. Makes 4 servings.

SHRIMP 'N SHELL CASSEROLE

1 can (10¾ ounces) condensed
   cream of celery soup
¼ cup milk
1 tablespoon sherry
½ teaspoon curry powder
1½ cups diced cooked shrimp
2 cups cooked shell macaroni
2 tablespoons chopped parsley

In 1-quart casserole, blend soup, milk, sherry, and curry powder. Add remaining ingredients. Bake at 350°F. for 30 minutes; stir. Makes about 3½ cups.

FRANK-POTATO BAKE

¼ cup chopped onion
1 tablespoon butter or margarine
1 can (10¾ ounces) condensed
   cream of celery soup
⅓ cup water
1 tablespoon prepared mustard
4 cups sliced cooked potatoes
6 frankfurters, slashed

In saucepan, cook onion in butter until tender; stir in soup, water, and mustard. Add potatoes. Pour into 1½-quart shallow baking dish (10x 6x2"); top with frankfurters. Bake at 400°F. for 25 minutes or until hot. Makes 4 servings.

SEAFOOD BAKE

1 can (10¾ ounces) condensed
   cream of mushroom soup
⅓ cup mayonnaise
⅓ cup milk
1 can (5 ounces) shrimp, drained
1 can (about 7 ounces) tuna,
   drained and flaked
½ cup sliced water chestnuts
1 cup finely chopped celery
2 tablespoons chopped parsley
2 teaspoons finely chopped onion
2 cups cooked macaroni
Paprika

In 1½-quart casserole, blend soup, mayonnaise, and milk. Add remaining ingredients except paprika. Bake at 350°F. for 30 minutes or until hot; stir. Sprinkle with paprika. Makes about 4 cups.

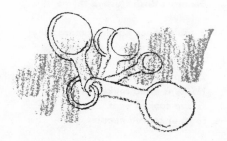

The Meat of the Matter

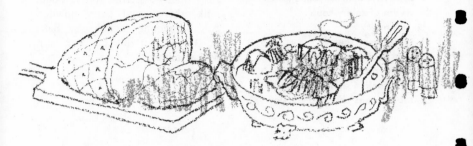

CALLING ALL BEEF-EATERS

What's the heavy-weight item in most food budgets? Meat. What's the champion dish at most meals? Meat again. And the meat that often merits the greatest applause is beef. Conscientious cooks are always on the lookout for ways to make the most of this perennial winner. For them, the following recipes. Each uses convenient condensed soup and each boasts serve-it-again flavor.

STEW 'N DUMPLINGS

¼ cup chopped onion
1 tablespoon butter or margarine
1 can (10¾ ounces) condensed vegetable soup
½ soup can water
1½ cups diced cooked beef
1 cup biscuit mix
⅓ cup milk

In saucepan, cook onion in butter until tender. Add soup, water, and beef. Bring to boil. Meanwhile, combine biscuit mix and milk. Drop 5 to 6 spoonfuls on boiling soup. Cook uncovered over low heat 10 minutes. Cover; cook 10 minutes more. Makes about 3 cups.

CREAMED COOKED BEEF

¼ cup thinly sliced celery
¼ cup chopped onion
Generous dash crushed thyme leaves
2 tablespoons butter or margarine
1 can (10¾ ounces) condensed cream of mushroom soup
⅓ cup water
1½ cups diced cooked beef
½ cup cooked peas
Toast or cooked noodles

In saucepan, cook celery and onion with thyme in butter until tender. Stir in remaining ingredients except toast. Heat; stir occasionally. Serve over toast. Makes about 3 cups.

SAUCY BEEF HASH

2 cups diced cooked beef
2 cups diced cooked potatoes
¼ cup finely chopped onion
4 tablespoons butter or margarine
1 can (10¾ ounces) condensed
   cream of celery soup
½ cup chopped parsley
1½ teaspoons Worcestershire
1 tablespoon ketchup
Dash pepper

In skillet, brown beef and potatoes and cook onion in butter until tender. Stir in remaining ingredients. Heat; stir occasionally. Makes about 3½ cups.

SWISS STEAK WITH VEGETABLES

1½ pounds round steak (¾" thick)
2 tablespoons shortening
1 can (10½ ounces) condensed
   onion soup
½ cup water
½ teaspoon salt
⅛ teaspoon pepper
4 medium carrots (about ½ pound),
   cut in 2-inch pieces
4 medium potatoes (about 1½
   pounds), cut in half
2 tablespoons flour
1 tablespoon chopped parsley

Pound meat; cut into serving-size pieces. In skillet, brown meat in shortening. Add soup, ¼ cup water, and seasonings. Cover; cook over low heat 30 minutes. Add carrots and potatoes. Cook 1 hour more or until tender. Stir occasionally. Gradually blend ¼ cup water into flour until smooth; slowly stir into sauce. Cook, stirring until thickened. Garnish with parsley. Makes 4 servings.

YANKEE POT ROAST

3 to 4-pound beef pot roast
1 can (10½ ounces) condensed
   onion soup
¼ cup water
2 to 4 tablespoons flour

In large heavy pan, brown beef (use shortening if necessary); pour off fat. Add soup. Cover; cook over low heat 2½ to 3 hours or until meat is done. Stir occasionally. Gradually blend water into flour until smooth; slowly stir into sauce. Cook, stirring until thickened. Makes 6 to 8 servings.

23

BARBECUED STEAK SUPREME

2 pounds boneless round steak
   (¾" thick)
3 tablespoons flour
2 tablespoons shortening
1 can (10¾ ounces) condensed
   tomato soup
⅓ cup chopped onion
⅓ cup chopped celery
1 small clove garlic, minced
1 tablespoon brown sugar
1 tablespoon Worcestershire
1 tablespoon lemon juice or vinegar
1 teaspoon prepared mustard
Generous dash hot pepper sauce
Cooked rice

Pound flour into meat; cut into serving-size pieces. In skillet, brown meat in shortening; pour off fat. Add remaining ingredients except rice. Cover; cook over low heat 1 hour 30 minutes. Stir occasionally. Serve with rice. Makes 6 servings.

SOUPER STROGANOFF

1½ pounds boneless round steak
   (¾" thick)
1 can (about 4 ounces) sliced
   mushrooms, drained
½ cup chopped onion
1 small clove garlic, minced
2 tablespoons butter or margarine
1 can (10½ ounces) condensed
   consommé
⅓ cup flour
1 cup sour cream
1 tablespoon chopped parsley
Cooked noodles

Freeze meat 1 hour to firm (makes slicing easier). Cut meat into *very* thin strips. In skillet, brown mushrooms and cook onion with garlic in butter until *just* tender; push to one side. Add meat. Cook until color changes (about 3 to 4 minutes). Blend consommé into flour until smooth; stir into meat mixture. Cook, stirring until thickened. Add sour cream and parsley; heat. Serve over noodles. Makes about 5 cups.

SMOTHERED STEAK ROLL-UPS

1½ pounds thinly sliced round
   steak (¼" thick)
1½ cups prepared packaged
   herb seasoned stuffing mix
2 tablespoons shortening
1 can (10¾ ounces) condensed
   cream of mushroom or
   golden mushroom soup
½ cup water

Cut steak into 6 pieces (about 8x4"). Pound with meat hammer. Place ¼ cup stuffing near center of each piece of meat. Roll up; tuck in ends and fasten with skewers or toothpicks. In skillet, brown roll-ups in shortening; pour off fat. Add soup and water. Cover; cook over low heat 1¼ hours or until tender. Stir occasionally. 6 servings.

TOMATO BEEF STEW

1½ pounds beef cubes (1½-inch)
2 tablespoons shortening
1 can (10¾ ounces) condensed
 tomato soup
½ cup water
6 small whole white onions
6 small carrots, cut in half
3 potatoes, quartered
¼ teaspoon thyme leaves, crushed

Brown meat in shortening in large heavy pan. Add soup and water. Cover; simmer 1½ hours. Add remaining ingredients. Cover; cook 1 hour or until vegetables are tender. Stir occasionally. Uncover; cook to desired consistency. Makes about 6 cups.

EASY SWISS STEAK

1½ pounds round steak
 (¾" thick)
2 tablespoons shortening
1 can (10¾ ounces) condensed
 golden mushroom soup
½ cup chopped canned tomatoes
¼ cup chopped onion
¼ cup water
Dash pepper

Pound steak; cut into serving-size pieces. In skillet, brown steak in shortening; pour off fat. Add remaining ingredients. Cover; cook over low heat 1 hour 30 minutes or until tender. Stir occasionally. Makes 4 to 6 servings.

NORSEMAN'S STEW

1½ pounds beef cubes (1½-inch)
2 tablespoons shortening
1 can (10¾ ounces) condensed
 golden mushroom soup
¼ cup water
½ cup chopped canned tomatoes
1 teaspoon wine vinegar
Generous dash cinnamon
2 whole cloves
1 pound (about 16) small whole
 white onions

In large heavy pan, brown beef in shortening; pour off fat. Stir in remaining ingredients except onions. Cover; cook over low heat 1½ hours. Add onions; cook 1 hour more or until meat is tender. Stir occasionally. Makes about 5 cups.

BEEFED-UP NOODLES 'N BEANS

1 pound round steak (¾" thick)
½ cup chopped onion
1 medium clove garlic, minced
½ teaspoon salt
⅛ teaspoon basil leaves, crushed
⅛ teaspoon pepper
2 tablespoons salad oil
1 can (10¾ ounces) condensed golden mushroom soup
1 can (15½ ounces) kidney beans, drained
2 cups cooked noodles
1 can (about 8 ounces) stewed tomatoes

Freeze meat 1 hour to firm (makes slicing easier); slice into *very* thin strips. In skillet, cook onion with seasonings in oil until *just* tender; push to one side. Add meat; cook until color changes (about 3 to 4 minutes). Add remaining ingredients. Heat; stir occasionally. Makes about 6 cups.

STEAK IN SAUCE

1½ pounds round steak (¾" thick)
2 tablespoons shortening
1 can (10½ ounces) condensed cream of mushroom soup
¼ cup water

Pound steak; cut in serving-size pieces. In skillet, brown steak in shortening; pour off fat. Add soup and water. Cover; cook over low heat 1 hour 30 minutes or until tender. Stir occasionally. Makes 4 to 6 servings.

SPICY SHORT RIBS

3 pounds short ribs, cut in serving-size pieces
1 can (10¾ ounces) condensed cream of chicken soup
½ cup wine vinegar
⅓ cup water
2 medium bay leaves
8 whole cloves
4 whole peppercorns
¾ cup water
⅓ cup crushed gingersnaps
2 tablespoons sugar
Spiced apple rings
Parsley

Place meat in deep bowl. Combine soup, vinegar, ⅓ cup water, bay leaves, cloves, and peppercorns; pour over meat. Cover; refrigerate 24 hours, turning meat twice. In large heavy pan, combine meat, soup marinade, and ¾ cup water. Cover; cook over low heat 2½ hours or until tender. Stir occasionally. Remove meat from pan; keep warm. Skim fat from sauce; remove bay leaves, cloves, peppercorns. Stir in gingersnaps and sugar. Cook, stirring until thickened. Serve with ribs. Garnish with apple rings and parsley. Makes 4 servings.

STROGANOFF STEW

3½-pound boned chuck roast
2 tablespoons shortening
2 cans (10¾ ounces each)
    condensed cream of mushroom
    soup
½ cup sour cream
½ cup water
1 teaspoon paprika
Generous dash pepper
1 pound medium carrots, halved
1 pound whole small white onions
Cooked wide noodles

Trim fat from meat and cut into 1-inch cubes. In large heavy pan, brown beef in shortening; pour off fat. Add soup, sour cream, water, paprika, and pepper. Cover; cook over low heat 1 hour. Add vegetables. Cover; cook over low heat 1 hour longer or until meat and vegetables are tender. Stir occasionally. Serve with noodles. Makes about 8 cups.

CHUNKY BEEF 'N NOODLES

1 can (about 2 ounces) sliced
    mushrooms, drained
¼ cup chopped onion
2 tablespoons butter or margarine
1 can (19 ounces) chunky beef soup
¼ cup sour cream
1 cup cooked noodles
2 teaspoons paprika

In saucepan, brown mushrooms and cook onion in butter until tender. Add remaining ingredients. Heat; stir occasionally. Makes about 3 cups.

PEPPER STEAK

1½ pounds round steak (¾" thick)
2 tablespoons shortening
1 can (10¾ ounces) condensed
    tomato soup
⅓ cup water
1 teaspoon lemon juice
½ cup green pepper strips

Pound steak; cut into serving-size pieces. In skillet, brown meat in shortening; pour off fat. Stir in soup, water, and lemon juice. Cover; cook over low heat 1 hour 15 minutes. Add pepper. Cook 15 minutes more or until meat is tender. Stir occasionally. 4 to 6 servings.

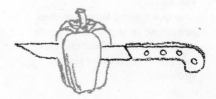

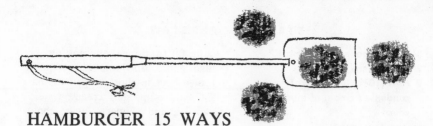

HAMBURGER 15 WAYS

Thank heaven for hamburger! Without it, what would thrifty cooks do? With it, there are a thousand delicious possibilities. Here are a few of them, all brightened by handy condensed soup. Bonus: Soup helps prevent shrinkage in meat loaves and burgers while contributing extra flavor.

SPREAD-A-BURGER

1 can (10¾ ounces) condensed
  tomato soup
1½ pounds ground beef
⅓ cup finely chopped onion
1 tablespoon prepared mustard
1 tablespoon Worcestershire
1 teaspoon salt
1 teaspoon prepared horseradish
Dash pepper
8 frankfurter buns, split and toasted
8 slices (8 ounces) process
  American cheese

Combine ⅓ cup soup with remaining ingredients except buns and cheese. Spread mixture evenly over bun halves; *cover edges completely.* Broil 4 inches from heat for 5 minutes or until done. Top with remaining soup and cheese. Broil until cheese melts. Makes 8 sandwiches.

MEATBALL STEW

1 pound ground beef
1 egg, slightly beaten
½ cup small bread cubes
¾ cup finely chopped onion
½ teaspoon salt
2 tablespoons shortening
1 can (10½ ounces) condensed
  beef broth
1 can (10¾ ounces) condensed
  tomato soup
⅛ teaspoon thyme leaves, crushed
1 can (about 16 ounces) small whole
  white potatoes, drained and cut up
1 can (16 ounces) sliced carrots,
  drained

Mix *thoroughly* beef, egg, bread cubes, ¼ cup onion, and salt. Shape *firmly* into 36 meatballs. In large saucepan, brown meatballs and cook remaining onion in shortening; pour off fat. Add remaining ingredients. Heat; stir occasionally. Makes about 6½ cups.

OLD-FASHIONED MEAT LOAF

1 can (10½ ounces) condensed
    vegetable soup
2 pounds ground beef
½ cup chopped onion
½ cup fine dry bread crumbs
1 egg, slightly beaten
1 teaspoon salt
Dash pepper

Combine all ingredients; mix *thoroughly*. Shape *firmly* into loaf (8x4x2½"); place in shallow baking pan. (*Thorough* mixing and *firm* shaping will produce a moist, easy-to-slice loaf.) Bake at 375°F. 1 hour 15 minutes. 6 servings. VARIATION: After loaf has baked 1 hour, garnish top with 4 tomato slices and ½ cup shredded mild cheese; bake 15 minutes more.

TOP-STOVE MEAT LOAF

1½ pounds ground beef
½ cup fine dry bread crumbs
1 can (10¾ ounces) condensed
    tomato soup
¼ cup finely chopped onion
1 egg, slightly beaten
1 teaspoon salt
Generous dash pepper
1 tablespoon shortening
¼ cup water
½ teaspoon prepared mustard
2 slices process cheese, cut in half

Mix *thoroughly* beef, crumbs, ¼ cup soup, onion, egg, and seasonings. Shape *firmly* into 2 loaves; brown on both sides in skillet in shortening (to turn loaves, use pancake turner). Cover; cook over low heat 25 minutes. Spoon off fat. Stir in remaining soup, water, mustard. Top loaves with cheese. Uncover; cook 10 minutes. 4 to 6 servings. *Oven Method:* Mix and shape as above. Bake at 350°F. for 40 minutes. Spoon off fat. Pour remaining soup (omit water) mixed with mustard on loaves; top with cheese. Bake until cheese melts.

SPAGHETTI WITH MEAT SAUCE

1 pound ground beef
1 cup chopped onion
2 large cloves garlic, minced
1 teaspoon oregano leaves, crushed
¼ teaspoon thyme leaves, crushed
2 cans (10¾ ounces each)
    condensed tomato soup
½ cup water
1 teaspoon salt
1 bay leaf
⅛ teaspoon pepper
Cooked spaghetti
Grated Parmesan cheese

In saucepan, brown beef and cook onion with garlic, oregano, and thyme until tender (use shortening if necessary). Stir to separate meat. Add remaining ingredients except spaghetti and cheese. Simmer 30 minutes; stir occasionally. Remove bay leaf. Serve over spaghetti with cheese. Makes about 4½ cups.

ONION BURGERS

1 pound ground beef
1 cup chopped celery
1 can (10½ ounces) condensed
  onion soup
¼ cup water
¼ cup ketchup
1 teaspoon Worcestershire
1 teaspoon prepared mustard
Dash pepper
Hamburger buns, split and toasted

In skillet, brown beef and cook celery until tender (use shortening if necessary). Stir to separate meat; pour off fat. Add remaining ingredients except buns. Cook over low heat 15 minutes. Stir occasionally. Serve on buns. Makes about 2½ cups.

HAMBURGERS ITALIANO

1 pound ground beef
½ teaspoon salt
Dash pepper
1 can (10¾ ounces) condensed
  tomato soup
1 can (2 ounces) sliced mushrooms,
  drained
1 small onion, sliced
¼ teaspoon oregano leaves,
  crushed
1 small clove garlic, minced

Combine beef, salt, and pepper; shape into 4 patties. In skillet, brown patties (use shortening if necessary); pour off fat. Add remaining ingredients. Cover; cook over low heat 20 minutes or until done. Stir occasionally. Makes 4 servings.

MEAT-SHELL PIE

1 can (10¾ ounces) condensed
  tomato soup
1½ pounds ground beef
1 teaspoon salt
1½ teaspoons chili powder
6 frankfurters, split
½ cup chopped onion
2 tablespoons butter or margarine
½ cup shredded process cheese
Grated Parmesan cheese

Place a double layer of foil on cookie sheet. Mix *thoroughly* ⅓ cup soup, beef, salt, and 1 teaspoon chili powder; pat out firmly into 11-inch circle about ½-inch thick on foil. Turn up edges of foil to catch fat. Firmly press frankfurters, cut side up, into meat in spoke fashion. In saucepan, cook onion with remaining chili in butter until tender; stir in remaining soup; spread over meat. Bake at 450°F. for 15 minutes. Spoon off fat. Sprinkle with cheeses; bake until melted. 6 servings.

MANY WAY MEATBALLS

1 pound ground beef
¼ cup fine dry bread crumbs
¼ cup minced onion
1 egg, slightly beaten
¼ teaspoon salt
1 can (11 ounces) condensed
  Cheddar cheese, cream of celery
  or mushroom soup
¼ cup water
2 tablespoons chopped parsley

Mix beef, bread crumbs, onion, egg, and salt; shape into 16 meatballs. In skillet, brown meatballs; pour off drippings. Stir in soup, water, and parsley. Cover; cook over low heat 20 minutes; stir often. Makes about 3½ cups.

STUFFED CABBAGE ROLLS

8 large cabbage leaves
1 pound ground beef
1 cup cooked rice
¼ cup chopped onion
1 egg, slightly beaten
1 teaspoon salt
¼ teaspoon pepper
1 can (10¾ ounces) condensed
  tomato soup

Cook cabbage leaves in boiling salted water a few minutes to soften; drain. Combine beef, rice, onion, egg, salt, and pepper with 2 tablespoons soup. Divide meat mixture among cabbage leaves; roll and secure with toothpicks or string. Place cabbage rolls in skillet; pour remaining soup over. Cover; cook over low heat about 40 minutes. Stir often, spooning sauce over rolls. 4 servings.

SOUPER SAUCY MEAT LOAF

1½ pounds ground beef
1 can (10¾ ounces) condensed
  cream of mushroom or
  tomato soup
1 cup small bread cubes
¼ cup finely chopped onion
1 egg, slightly beaten
½ teaspoon salt
Generous dash pepper
¼ cup water

Mix *thoroughly* beef, ½ cup soup, bread, onion, egg, salt, and pepper. Shape *firmly* into loaf; place in shallow baking pan. Bake at 350°F. for 1 hour 15 minutes. Blend remaining soup, water, and 2 to 3 tablespoons drippings. Heat; stir occasionally. Serve over loaf. 4 to 6 servings.

ROLL-IN-ONE MEAT LOAF

1 can (10¾ ounces) condensed
   tomato soup
1½ pounds ground beef
½ cup fine dry bread crumbs
¼ cup minced onion
2 tablespoons chopped parsley
1 egg, slightly beaten
1 teaspoon salt
Dash pepper
1 package (9 ounces) frozen cut
   green beans, cooked,
   well-drained

Combine ½ cup soup with all ingredients except beans. Mix well. On waxed paper, pat into a 12x9-inch shape. Spread beans to within 1 inch of all edges; pat into meat. With aid of waxed paper, roll meat tightly, jelly-roll fashion, starting at long edge. Seal ends; use waxed paper to transfer to baking dish. Bake at 350°F. for 40 minutes. Spoon off fat. Pour remaining soup over loaf. Bake 10 minutes longer. 6 servings.

SWEDISH MEATBALLS

1 pound ground beef
¼ cup fine dry bread crumbs
¼ cup finely chopped onion
1 egg, slightly beaten
2 tablespoons chopped parsley
1 can (10¾ ounces) condensed
   cream of celery soup
½ cup water
¼ cup finely chopped dill pickle
Cooked rice

Mix thoroughly beef, bread crumbs, onion, egg, and parsley; shape into 16 meatballs. In skillet, brown meatballs (use shortening if necessary); pour off fat. Stir in soup, water, and pickle. Cover; cook over low heat 20 minutes or until done. Stir occasionally. Serve with rice. Makes about 3½ cups.

STUFFED PEPPERS

4 medium green peppers
1 pound ground beef
½ cup chopped onion
1 can (10¾ ounces) condensed
   tomato soup
1 cup cooked rice
2 teaspoons Worcestershire
½ teaspoon salt
Generous dash pepper
2 slices (2 ounces) mild process
   cheese, cut in strips

Remove tops and seeds from peppers; cook in boiling salted water about 5 minutes; drain. In skillet, brown beef and cook onion until tender (use shortening if necessary). Stir to separate meat; pour off fat. Stir in 1 cup soup, rice, and seasonings. Spoon meat mixture into peppers; arrange in 1½-quart casserole. Bake at 375°F. for 25 minutes. Top with remaining soup and cheese. Bake until cheese melts. Makes 4 servings.

Meatball Stew   Page 28
Norseman's Stew   Page 25

1 pound ground beef
¼ cup chopped onion
¼ cup chopped green pepper
1 can (10¾ ounces) condensed
   vegetable soup
½ teaspoon salt
⅛ teaspoon thyme leaves, crushed
2 cups seasoned mashed potatoes

In skillet, brown beef and cook onion and green pepper until tender (use shortening if necessary). Stir to separate meat; pour off fat. Stir in soup, salt, and thyme. Pour into 1½-quart casserole; spoon mashed potatoes around edge of casserole. Bake at 400°F. for 25 minutes or until hot. Makes about 3 cups.

PORK TO PERFECTION

Who doesn't adore the down-home flavor and hearty aroma of pork? Rich in protein and B vitamins, this popular meat plays many main dish roles. The following recipes call on condensed soups to enhance its versatility with exciting color and taste appeal.

GOLDEN PORK LOIN

3 to 4-pound pork loin rib roast
2 tablespoons shortening
1 can (10¾ ounces) condensed
   golden mushroom soup
½ cup water
½ cup chopped onion
1 tablespoon paprika
1 medium bay leaf
½ teaspoon salt
Dash pepper
6 medium carrots (about ¾ pound),
   cut in 2-inch pieces
4 medium potatoes (about 1½
   pounds), cut in half

In large heavy pan, brown meat in shortening; pour off fat. Add soup, water, onion, and seasonings. Cover; cook over low heat 1 hour 15 minutes. Stir occasionally. Add carrots and potatoes. Cook 1 hour more or until meat and vegetables are done. Remove bay leaf. Thicken sauce if desired. Makes 4 to 6 servings.

Skillet Franks
'n Noodles   Page 11

GLAZED FRUITED PORK CHOPS

6 pork chops (about 1½ pounds)
1 can (10½ ounces) condensed
  beef broth
1 tablespoon brown sugar
6 apple slices
6 orange slices
Dash ground cinnamon
Dash ground cloves
2 tablespoons orange juice
2 tablespoons cornstarch
Cooked rice

In skillet, brown chops (use shortening if necessary); pour off fat. Add broth and brown sugar. Cover; cook over low heat 15 minutes. Place an apple and orange slice on each chop; sprinkle with cinnamon and cloves. Cook over low heat 15 minutes more or until tender. Mix orange juice and cornstarch until smooth; gradually blend into sauce. Cook, stirring until thickened. Serve with rice. Makes 4 servings.

HAM BAKE

1½ cups diced cooked ham
2 tablespoons chopped onion
⅛ teaspoon tarragon leaves,
  crushed
2 tablespoons butter or margarine
1 can (10¾ ounces) condensed
  cream of chicken soup
½ cup water
2 cups cooked noodles
1 cup cooked French style
  green beans
2 tablespoons fine dry bread crumbs
1 small clove garlic, minced

In saucepan, brown ham and cook onion with tarragon in 1 tablespoon butter until tender. Stir in soup, water, noodles, and green beans. Pour into 1-quart casserole. Bake at 350°F. for 25 minutes or until hot; stir. Meanwhile, lightly brown crumbs with garlic in 1 tablespoon butter; sprinkle on casserole. Bake 5 minutes more. Makes about 3½ cups.

HURRY-UP PORK HASH

½ cup chopped onion
2 tablespoons butter or margarine
1 can (10¾ ounces) condensed
  cream of mushroom soup
¼ cup milk
1 teaspoon Worcestershire
1½ cups cubed cooked pork
2 cups cubed cooked potatoes
  (about 2 medium)
1 cup cooked peas

In skillet, cook onion in butter until tender. Stir in soup, milk, and Worcestershire. Add remaining ingredients. Heat; stir occasionally. Makes about 4 cups.

GLORIFIED CHOPS

6 pork chops (about 1½ pounds)
1 can (10¾ ounces) condensed
   cream of celery, mushroom, or
   golden mushroom or tomato soup
¼ to ⅓ cup water

In skillet, brown chops. Pour off fat. Stir in soup, water. Cover; cook over low heat 30 minutes or until tender. Stir occasionally. Makes 4 servings.

CREAMY BAKED CHOPS

Brown chops in oven-proof skillet as above. After adding liquids, cover; bake at 350°F. for 45 minutes or until tender.

PORK CHOPS 'N STUFFING

6 pork chops (about 1½ pounds)
6 cups soft bread cubes
½ cup finely chopped onion
4 tablespoons melted butter or
   margarine
⅔ cup water
¼ teaspoon poultry seasoning
1 can (10¾ ounces) condensed
   cream of mushroom soup

In skillet, brown pork chops (use shortening if necessary). Arrange in 2-quart shallow baking dish (12x8x 2″). Lightly toss bread cubes, onion, butter, ⅓ cup water, and poultry seasoning; spoon on chops. Bake at 350°F. for 30 minutes. Meanwhile, blend soup and ⅓ cup water; pour over chops. Bake 15 minutes more or until chops are tender. Makes 4 servings.

PORK CHOP AND POTATO SCALLOP

1 can (10¾ ounces) condensed
   cream of mushroom soup
½ cup sour cream
¼ cup water
½ teaspoon dried dill leaves,
   crushed
4 cups thinly sliced potatoes
4 pork chops (about 1 pound)
Salt
Pepper
Parsley

Blend soup, sour cream, water, and dill. In 2-quart casserole, alternate layers of potatoes and sauce; cover. Bake at 375°F. for 30 minutes. Meanwhile, in skillet, brown chops; season with salt and pepper. Arrange chops on potato mixture. Cover; bake 45 minutes more or until done. Garnish with parsley. Makes 3 servings.

LAMB, VEAL, LIVER

Variety is a virtue, especially at mealtime. So don that halo and whip up something different using these often-neglected meats. How about a tomatoey Lamb Ragout studded with cabbage wedges, potatoes, and caraway seed? Or liver simmered in condensed onion soup and chili sauce, then garnished with bacon? Interesting. Delicious. Easy.

LAMB KABOBS

¼ cup finely chopped onion
1 medium clove garlic, minced
1 teaspoon curry powder
⅛ teaspoon ground ginger
2 tablespoons butter or margarine
1 can (10¾ ounces) condensed cream of mushroom soup
¼ cup water
2 apples, quartered
1 medium green pepper, cut in 1½-inch pieces
1 pound lamb cubes for kabobs (1½-inch)

In saucepan, cook onion with garlic, curry, and ginger in butter until tender. Add soup and water. Simmer 5 minutes; stir occasionally. On 2 skewers, arrange alternately, apple and green pepper. On 2 separate skewers, arrange lamb; place lamb kabobs on broiler pan. Broil 4 inches from heat 5 minutes, turning and brushing with sauce. Add apple and green pepper kabobs. Cook 10 minutes more or until desired doneness, turning and brushing with sauce. Thin remaining sauce to desired consistency with water; heat. Serve with kabobs. Makes 4 servings.

MUSHROOM-LAMB CURRY

1½ pounds lamb cubes (1½-inch)
2 tablespoons shortening
½ cup chopped onion
½ cup chopped green pepper
½ cup chopped celery
1 large clove garlic, minced
2 teaspoons curry powder
1 can (10¾ ounces) condensed cream of mushroom soup
¼ cup water
Cooked rice

In skillet, brown lamb in shortening; pour off fat. Add remaining ingredients except rice. Cover; cook over low heat 1 hour 30 minutes or until meat is tender. Stir occasionally. Serve over rice. Makes about 3½ cups.

GRANDMOTHER'S LAMB STEW

1½ pounds lamb cubes (1½-inch)
2 tablespoons shortening
1 can (10½ ounces) condensed
  onion soup
1 cup diced celery
½ cup chopped canned tomatoes
1 medium clove garlic, minced
½ teaspoon salt
¼ teaspoon pepper
¼ teaspoon thyme leaves, crushed
4 medium potatoes (about
  1½ pounds), quartered
1 package (9 ounces) frozen cut
  green beans
2 tablespoons water
1 tablespoon flour

In large heavy pan, brown lamb in shortening; pour off fat. Add soup, celery, tomatoes, and seasonings. Cover; cook over low heat 1 hour. Add potatoes; cook 15 minutes more. Add green beans; cook 15 minutes more or until meat and vegetables are tender. Gradually blend water into flour until smooth; slowly stir into sauce. Cook, stirring until thickened. Makes about 8 cups.

LAMB RAGOUT

1½ pounds lamb cubes (1½-inch)
2 tablespoons shortening
1 can (10¾ ounces) condensed
  tomato soup
½ cup water
1 teaspoon salt
⅛ teaspoon pepper
⅛ teaspoon caraway seed
1 small clove garlic, minced
3 medium potatoes, cut in half
  (about 1 pound)
1 small head cabbage (about
  1 pound), cut in 4 wedges

In large heavy pan, brown lamb in shortening; pour off fat. Add soup, water, and seasonings. Cover; cook over low heat 30 minutes. Stir occasionally. Add potatoes; arrange cabbage on top. Cook 1 hour more or until meat and vegetables are tender. Makes 4 servings.

MINTED LEG OF LAMB

4-pound leg of lamb, boned
  and rolled
2 tablespoons orange marmalade
1 can (10¾ ounces) condensed
  golden mushroom soup
⅓ cup water
1 teaspoon dried mint leaves,
  crushed

Place lamb on rack in shallow baking pan, fat side up. Roast at 325°F. 2 hours 20 minutes or until done (35 to 40 minutes per pound or 175°F. on meat thermometer). Spread marmalade on meat last 30 minutes of roasting. Remove meat from pan. Spoon off excess fat, saving drippings. In roasting pan, add remaining ingredients to drippings. Heat, stirring to loosen browned bits. Serve with lamb. 4 to 6 servings.

HEARTY WINTER STEW

1½ pounds well-trimmed lamb
   cubes (about 1½-inch)
2 tablespoons shortening
1 can (10¾ ounces) condensed
   cream of chicken soup
1 can (16 ounces) tomatoes,
   chopped and drained
¼ teaspoon rosemary leaves,
   crushed
1 small clove garlic, minced
2 tablespoons mint jelly
1 pound rutabagas, cubed
6 medium carrots (about ¾ pound),
   cut in 2-inch pieces
8 small whole white onions
   (about ½ pound)

In large heavy pan, brown lamb in shortening; pour off fat. Add soup, tomatoes, seasonings, and jelly. Cover; cook over low heat 30 minutes. Add rutabagas, carrots, and onions. Cover; cook 1 hour more or until meat and vegetables are tender. Stir occasionally. Thicken sauce if desired. Makes about 5 cups.

VEAL BIRDS

1 pound thinly sliced veal cutlet
1 cup cooked rice
2 tablespoons butter or margarine
2 tablespoons chopped parsley
2 tablespoons shortening
2 tablespoons chopped onion
1 can (11 ounces) condensed
   tomato rice soup
¼ cup water
⅛ teaspoon leaf oregano, if desired

Pound veal with meat hammer; cut into 4 large or 8 small pieces. Combine rice, butter, and parsley; place a small amount on each piece of veal; roll and fasten with toothpicks or skewers. Brown veal birds in shortening along with onion; pour off excess drippings. Combine remaining ingredients; pour over meat. Cover; cook over low heat for 45 minutes. Spoon sauce over meat occasionally. 4 servings. Thin sauce to desired consistency with small amount of water before serving.

SAVORY LIVER SKILLET

1 pound sliced beef or calves liver,
   cut in strips
2 tablespoons flour
1 medium onion, sliced
2 tablespoons butter or margarine
1 can (10¾ ounces) condensed
   tomato soup
2 tablespoons water
½ cup green pepper strips
Cooked rice or noodles

Dust liver with flour. In skillet, brown liver and cook onion in butter. Add soup, water, and green pepper. Cover; cook over low heat 15 minutes or until liver is tender. Stir occasionally. Serve over rice. Makes about 3 cups.

CHICKEN LIVERS INDIENNE

1 package (8 ounces) frozen chicken
   livers, thawed
½ cup sliced celery
⅓ cup chopped onion
1 teaspoon curry powder
2 tablespoons butter or margarine
1 can (10¾ ounces) condensed
   golden mushroom soup
⅓ cup water
Cooked rice

In saucepan, cook livers, celery, onion, and curry in butter until livers are done. Stir in soup and water. Heat; stir occasionally. Serve over rice. Makes about 2 cups.

CHILI LIVER

4 slices bacon
1 pound sliced beef or calves liver
2 tablespoons flour
1 can (10½ ounces) condensed
   onion soup
¼ cup chili sauce or ketchup

In skillet, cook bacon until crisp; remove and crumble. Pour off fat, reserving 2 tablespoons drippings. Dust liver with flour; brown in drippings. Add soup and chili sauce. Cover; cook over low heat 15 minutes or until tender. Stir occasionally. Uncover; cook to desired consistency. Garnish with bacon. 4 servings.

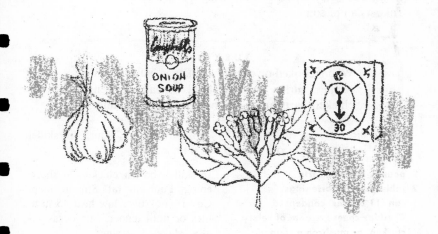

Poultry

Roast it, fry it, broil it, stew it, braise it, bake it. Any way you like it, poultry can't be beat—for versatility, taste, economy. What's more, there's a whole new world of poultry dishes waiting in cans of condensed soups, from hurry-up favorites to elegant company fare.

Take chicken. You can sauce it in the skillet, smother it in the baking dish, or simmer it in the pot. All with a variety of soups.

Take turkey. Its second-act appearance can be every bit as appealing as the first. Turkey Divan or A la King will see to that.

Take a can of soup . . .

TURKEY

Where cooked or canned chicken is indicated in recipes, turkey may be used instead. Frozen chicken parts are to be thawed before cooking.

GLORIFIED CHICKEN

2 pounds chicken parts
2 tablespoons shortening
1 can (11 ounces) condensed Cheddar cheese, cream of celery, chicken, or mushroom soup

In skillet, brown chicken in shortening. Pour off fat. Stir in soup. Cover; cook over low heat 45 minutes or until tender. Stir occasionally. Makes 4 servings.

PENTHOUSE CHICKEN
(pictured on cover)

2 pounds chicken parts
¼ cup seasoned flour
Shortening or salad oil
½ medium green pepper,
   cut in strips
½ cup sliced onion
⅛ to ¼ teaspoon thyme, crushed
1 can (10¾ ounces) condensed
   tomato soup
¼ cup water
1 teaspoon vinegar

ONE-STEP METHOD:

Dust chicken with seasoned flour. Brown in skillet in hot shortening (¼-inch deep). Cover; cook over low heat 45 minutes. Uncover last 10 minutes to crisp. Remove chicken to heated platter; keep warm. Pour off all but 2 tablespoons fat. Add green pepper, onion, and thyme; cook until green pepper is tender. Add remaining ingredients. Heat; stir occasionally. Serve over chicken. 4 servings.

Omit flour and water. Brown chicken in 2 tablespoons shortening. Pour off fat. Sprinkle with salt, pepper. Add remaining ingredients (increase vinegar to 1 tablespoon). Cover; cook over low heat 45 minutes or until tender. Stir occasionally.

CHICKEN KETTLE

1 can (10¾ ounces) condensed
   cream of chicken soup
¾ cup water
1 cup sliced celery
1 medium onion, quartered
2 teaspoons salt
½ teaspoon poultry seasoning
¼ teaspoon pepper
4 to 5-pound stewing chicken,
   cut up
4 medium potatoes (about 1
   pound), quartered
6 small carrots (about ¾ pound),
   cut in 2-inch pieces
¼ cup flour

In large heavy pan, combine soup, ¼ cup water, celery, onion, and seasonings; add chicken. Cover; cook over low heat 1 hour 30 minutes. Stir occasionally. Add potatoes and carrots. Cook 45 minutes more or until chicken and vegetables are tender. Remove chicken and vegetables to serving platter. Gradually blend remaining ½ cup water into flour until smooth; slowly stir into sauce. Cook, stirring until thickened. Makes 6 servings.

TURKEY DIVAN
(also Chicken Divan)

1 package (10 ounces) frozen
   broccoli or asparagus spears,
   cooked and drained
4 servings sliced cooked turkey
   or chicken
1 can (10¾ ounces) condensed
   cream of celery, chicken, or
   mushroom soup
⅓ cup milk
½ cup shredded Cheddar cheese

Arrange broccoli in shallow baking dish (10x6x2"). Top with turkey slices. Blend soup and milk; pour over turkey; sprinkle with cheese. Bake in a 450° oven until sauce is slightly browned, about 15 minutes. 4 servings.

POULET AU VIN

2 pounds chicken parts
2 tablespoons shortening
1 can (10¾ ounces) condensed
  cream of mushroom soup
¼ cup sherry
8 small whole white onions
  (about ½ pound)

In skillet, brown chicken in shortening; pour off fat. Stir in soup and sherry; add onions. Cover; cook over low heat 45 minutes or until tender. Stir occasionally. 4 servings.

GOLDEN CHICKEN BAKE

2 pounds chicken parts
2 tablespoons melted butter or
  margarine
1 can (11 ounces) condensed
  Cheddar cheese, cream of celery,
  chicken, or mushroom soup
¼ cup chopped toasted almonds

In shallow baking dish (12x8x2"), arrange chicken skin-side down. Pour butter over. Bake at 400°F. for 20 minutes. Turn chicken; bake 20 minutes more. Stir soup; pour over chicken; sprinkle with almonds. Bake 20 minutes more or until tender. Stir sauce before serving. 4 servings.

CHICKEN CROQUETTES WITH SAUCE

1 can (10¾ ounces) condensed
  cream of chicken soup
1½ cups finely chopped cooked
  chicken
¼ cup fine dry bread crumbs
2 tablespoons finely chopped
  parsley
1 tablespoon finely chopped onion
Shortening
½ cup milk

Combine ⅓ cup soup, chicken, bread crumbs, parsley, and onion. Mix well; shape into 6 croquettes or patties (if mixture is difficult to handle, chill before shaping). Roll in additional bread crumbs. In skillet, brown croquettes in shortening. Meanwhile, in saucepan, combine remaining soup and milk. Heat; stir occasionally. Serve with croquettes. Makes 3 servings.

CREAMED CHICKEN

½ cup chopped celery
2 tablepoons butter or margarine
1 can (10¾ ounces) condensed
  cream of chicken soup
½ cup milk
1 can (5 ounces) boned chicken
  or turkey, cut up
1 cup cooked peas
Generous dash ground sage
Biscuits, corn bread, toast,
  or cooked noodles

In saucepan, cook celery in butter until tender; blend in soup and milk. Add chicken, peas, and sage. Heat; stir occasionally. Serve over biscuits. Makes about 3 cups.

CHICKEN A LA KING

¼ cup chopped onion
2 tablespoons chopped green
  pepper
2 tablespoons butter or margarine
1 can (10¾ ounces) condensed
  cream of chicken or
  mushroom soup
⅓ to ½ cup milk
1½ cups cubed cooked chicken,
  ham, or turkey
2 tablespoons diced pimiento
Dash pepper
Toast

Cook onion and green pepper in butter until tender. Blend in soup and milk; add chicken, pimiento, and pepper. Heat slowly; stir often. Serve over toast. Makes about 2½ cups.

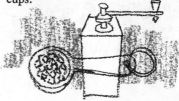

CHICKEN LIVERS IN PATTY SHELLS

1 package (8 ounces) frozen
  chicken livers, thawed
½ cup chopped celery
¼ cup chopped onion
2 tablespoons butter or margarine
1 can (10¾ ounces) condensed
  cream of chicken soup
½ cup milk
¼ teaspoon paprika
Patty shells or toast

In skillet, cook livers, celery, and onion in butter until livers are done. Blend in soup, milk, and paprika. Heat; stir occasionally. Serve in patty shells. Makes about 2 cups.

PARTY CHICKEN

2 pounds chicken parts
2 tablespoons shortening
1 can (10¾ ounces) condensed
  chicken broth
1 can (4 ounces) mushroom
  buttons, drained
⅓ cup Burgundy or other dry
  red wine
10 small whole white onions
  (about 10 ounces)
1 bay leaf
1 large clove garlic, minced
¼ teaspoon thyme, crushed
½ cup water
¼ cup flour

In skillet, brown chicken in shortening; pour off fat. Add broth, mushrooms, wine, onions, bay leaf, garlic, and thyme. Cover; cook over low heat 45 minutes or until chicken and onions are tender. Stir occasionally. Remove bay leaf. Gradually blend water into flour until smooth; slowly stir into sauce. Cook, stirring until thickened. 4 servings.

Savory Stuffings

Feel like feasting? Call on stuffing. It's guaranteed to glorify even ordinary fare. Served with fowl, fish, chops, or simply as a sidedish, dressings like the following are a credit to any cook's reputation.

OLD-FASHIONED POULTRY STUFFING

1 cup chopped celery
½ cup finely chopped onion
1 teaspoon poultry seasoning
⅛ teaspoon pepper
4 tablespoons butter or margarine
1 can (10¾ ounces) condensed
    cream of chicken soup
8 cups dry bread cubes

In skillet, cook celery and onion with seasonings in butter until tender. Add soup. Toss lightly with bread cubes. Spoon into a 1½-quart casserole. Bake at 350°F. for 45 minutes. Makes 6 cups stuffing or enough for a 5 to 6-pound bird.

OVERSTUFFED CHICKEN

2 cans (10¾ ounces each)
    condensed golden mushroom soup
⅔ cup water
1 package (8 ounces) herb seasoned
    stuffing mix
2 broilers (about 2½ pounds each),
    split
Paprika
⅓ cup chopped onion
Generous dash poultry seasoning
2 tablespoons butter or margarine

Combine soup with water. In roasting pan (15x10½"), mix ⅔ cup soup mixture with stuffing mix; spread in pan. Arrange broilers over stuffing; sprinkle with paprika. Cover; bake at 400°F. for 30 minutes. Uncover; bake 45 minutes longer or until tender. Meanwhile, in saucepan, cook onion with seasoning in butter until onion is tender. Stir in remaining soup mixture. Heat; stir occasionally. Serve with chicken and stuffing. 4 servings.

OYSTER STUFFING

¼ cup chopped celery
2 tablespoons chopped onion
¼ teaspoon sage
2 tablespoons butter or margarine
1 can (10½ ounces) condensed
  oyster stew
8 cups dry bread cubes

In saucepan, cook celery and onion with sage in butter until tender. Add soup. Toss lightly with bread cubes. Spoon into 1½-quart casserole. Bake at 350°F. for 45 minutes. Makes 6 cups stuffing.

SAVORY SAUSAGE STUFFING

½ pound bulk sausage
1 small onion, chopped
1 can (10¾ ounces) condensed
  cream of celery soup
8 cups dry bread cubes

In skillet, brown sausage and cook onion until tender; stir to separate meat. Pour off fat. Blend in soup; toss lightly with bread cubes. Spoon into a 1½-quart casserole. Bake at 350°F. for 45 minutes. Makes 6½ cups stuffing or enough for a 5 to 6-pound bird.

DEEP SOUTH STUFFING

1 cup chopped celery
½ cup chopped onion
2 tablespoons butter or margarine
1 can (10¾ ounces) condensed
  cream of chicken soup
6 cups dry bread cubes
2 cups coarse corn bread crumbs
1 egg, slightly beaten
1 teaspoon poultry seasoning

In skillet, cook celery and onion in butter until tender. Add soup, bread cubes, corn bread, egg, and poultry seasoning; toss lightly. Makes 6 cups stuffing or enough for a 5 to 6-pound bird.

DUTCH COUNTRY STUFFING

1 can (10½ ounces) condensed
  beef broth
2 cups chopped apple
¾ cup chopped onion
½ cup chopped celery
¼ cup sugar
2 tablespoons butter or margarine
¼ teaspoon ground sage
⅛ teaspoon ground nutmeg
Dash ground cinnamon
12 cups dry bread cubes

In saucepan, combine all ingredients except bread cubes; simmer 10 minutes. Pour over bread cubes a little at a time, mixing well after each addition. Makes 8 cups or enough stuffing for a 5 to 6-pound pork shoulder roast.

Fish and Seafood

Here's one fish story you can believe: Seafood is never better than when it's teamed with a zesty sauce. And sauce-making is never easier than when it begins with a can of soup.

Whether you catch your fish in the freezer or offshore, these recipes will bring them to the table looking and tasting sensational.

SAUCY FISH FILLETS

1 pound fish fillets
Generous dash pepper
1 can (10¾ ounces) condensed
  cream of celery soup
½ cup shredded mild process cheese
Generous dash paprika

Arrange fillets in single layer in shallow baking dish (10x6x2"); sprinkle with pepper. Bake at 350°F. for 15 minutes. Pour soup over, stirring into liquid around fish. Sprinkle with cheese and paprika. Bake 10 minutes more or until done. Stir before serving. Garnish with parsley or lemon wedges if desired. 3 servings.

SEASIDE STEW

1 can (4 ounces) sliced mushrooms,
  drained
1 tablespoon butter or margarine
1 can (10¾ ounces) condensed
  cream of celery soup
½ cup milk
2 cups diced cooked seafood
  (crab meat, shrimp, scallops, fish)
¼ cup shredded sharp Cheddar
  cheese
3 tablespoons sauterne or other
  dry white wine

In saucepan, brown mushrooms in butter. Add remaining ingredients. Heat until cheese melts; stir occasionally. Serve over rice. Garnish with paprika and parsley. Makes about 3½ cups.

SHRIMP A LA KING

1 can (4 ounces) sliced mushrooms,
   drained
¼ cup chopped onion
2 tablespoons butter or margarine
1 can (11 ounces) condensed
   Cheddar cheese soup
½ cup milk
1 cup diced cooked shrimp
Rice or toast

In saucepan, brown mushrooms and cook onion in butter until tender. Add soup, milk, and shrimp. Heat; stir occasionally. Serve over rice. Makes about 2½ cups.

SHRIMP CREOLE

1 large green pepper, cut in strips
1 large onion, sliced
1 large clove garlic, minced
2 tablespoons butter or margarine
1 can (10¾ ounces) condensed
   tomato soup
2 teaspoons lemon juice
⅛ teaspoon hot pepper sauce
4 cups frozen cleaned raw shrimp
   (about 12 ounces)
2 teaspoons water
1 teaspoon cornstarch
Cooked rice

In saucepan, cook green pepper and onion with garlic in butter until tender. Add soup, lemon juice, and hot pepper sauce. Bring to boil. Add shrimp. Reduce heat. Simmer 5 minutes or until shrimp is done. Stir occasionally. Meanwhile, blend water into cornstarch until smooth; slowly stir into sauce. Cook, stirring until thickened. Serve over rice. Makes about 3½ cups.

LOBSTER-SHRIMP THERMIDOR

1 can (4 ounces) sliced mushrooms,
   drained
1 tablespoon butter or margarine
1 can (10¾ ounces) condensed
   cream of celery soup
¼ cup milk
1 cup diced cooked lobster
½ cup diced cooked shrimp
¼ teaspoon dry mustard
Dash cayenne pepper
Grated Parmesan cheese
Paprika

In saucepan, brown mushrooms in butter. Add soup, milk, seafood, mustard, and cayenne. Spoon into 4 individual baking dishes; sprinkle with cheese and paprika. Bake at 400°F. for 15 minutes or until hot. 4 servings.

GRATIN OF OYSTERS AND SPINACH

2 tablespoons sliced green onion
1 tablespoon butter or margarine
1 can (10½ ounces) condensed oyster stew
1 soup can milk
2 slices (about 2 ounces) Canadian bacon, cut in strips
½ cup cooked chopped spinach
¼ cup shredded Swiss cheese

In saucepan, cook onion in butter until tender. Add remaining ingredients. Heat until cheese melts; stir occasionally. Makes about 3 cups.

BARBECUE-BAKED FISH

1 pound fish fillets (thaw if frozen)
1 tablespoon butter or margarine
4 thin slices lemon
4 thin onion rings
2 tablespoons chopped parsley
1 can (10¾ ounces) condensed tomato soup

In baking dish (10x6x2") place fish; sprinkle with salt, pepper. Dot with butter; top with lemon, onion, parsley. Bake at 350°F. for 15 minutes. Pour soup over, stirring in liquid around fish. Bake 10 minutes more or until done. Stir before serving. 3 servings.

DEVILED CRAB

1 can (10¾ ounces) condensed cream of celery soup
1 cup flaked cooked crab meat, or 1 can (7 ounces), drained
2 tablespoons chopped green pepper
1 tablespoon chopped onion
2 teaspoons lemon juice
1 teaspoon Worcestershire
½ teaspoon prepared mustard
2 tablespoons buttered bread crumbs

Combine all ingredients, except bread crumbs; spoon into 4 small buttered baking dishes. (Clam shells are attractive for this.) Sprinkle crumbs over crab mixture. Bake in a 350° oven 20 minutes or until lightly browned. 2 to 3 servings.

OYSTERS A LA QUEEN

1 can (4 ounces) sliced mushrooms, drained
¼ cup chopped onion
2 tablespoons butter or margarine
2 tablespoons flour
1 can (10½ ounces) condensed oyster stew
¼ cup milk
2 tablespoons diced pimiento

In saucepan, brown mushrooms and cook onion in butter until tender. Blend in flour; gradually stir in stew, milk, and pimiento. Heat, stirring until thickened. Makes about 2 cups. Serve over cooked chicken, fish, broccoli spears, or asparagus spears.

CREAMED SALMON

¼ cup chopped onion
1 tablespoon butter or margarine
1 can (10¾ ounces) condensed cream of mushroom soup
⅓ cup milk
1 tablespoon lemon juice
1 can (about 8 ounces) salmon, drained and flaked
1 cup cooked cut green beans
Toast

In saucepan, cook onion in butter until tender. Blend in remaining ingredients except toast. Heat; stir occasionally. Serve over toast. Makes about 2½ cups.

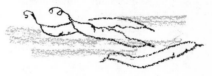

SEAFOOD AU GRATIN

1 can (11 ounces) condensed Cheddar cheese soup
¼ cup milk
2 cups cooked cut up seafood (shrimp, lobster, crab meat, fish)
1 tablespoon chopped parsley
¼ cup buttered bread crumbs

In 1-quart casserole, stir soup; gradually add milk. Stir in seafood and parsley. Bake at 350°F. for 25 minutes or until hot; stir. Top with bread crumbs. Bake 5 minutes more. Makes about 3 cups.

HUNGARIAN SHRIMP

1 can (10¾ ounces) condensed cream of mushroom soup
½ cup sour cream
¼ cup water
1½ cups diced cooked shrimp
⅛ teaspoon paprika
Cooked noodles

In saucepan, combine all ingredients except noodles. Heat; stir occasionally. Serve over noodles. Makes about 2½ cups.

Saucery

Lucky the cook who discovers the versatile sauces always on hand in cans of condensed soup. Whether you're adding new flavor appeal to leftover meat or preparing gravy for chicken, a can of soup is ready to fill your sauce-making needs with remarkable ease.

White or cream sauce comes already blended in a can of cream soup. Choose the one with the special flavor you want—cream of chicken, mushroom, or celery soup. Simply add a little liquid to achieve the consistency you prefer and use it as a pour-on or in recipes. For gravy, just blend cream soups with some liquid and/or drippings. Delectable.

Tomato sauce, cheese sauce, golden mushroom sauce—these, too, are at your fingertips when you open a can of soup. Bon Appetit.

VERSATILE CREAM SAUCE

1 can (10¾ ounces) condensed
   cream of celery, chicken, or
   mushroom soup
¼ cup milk

Pour soup into pan. Stir to blend. Add milk. Heat; stir often. Makes about 1½ cups sauce. Use for creaming vegetables and meats.

INSTANT CHEESE SAUCE: Pour 1 can Cheddar cheese soup into pan. Stir contents well to blend. Stir in ¼ to ⅓ cup milk. Heat slowly, stirring often.

4-WAY CHEESE SAUCE: Pour 1 can any cream soup into pan. Stir to blend. Add ¼ to ½ cup milk and ½ cup shredded Cheddar cheese. Heat; stir often.

Type Sauce	Use 1 can Soup	Add and Heat
Almond for chicken, veal, seafood	Cream of chicken or mushroom	¼ cup milk, ¼ cup chopped almonds and 1 tablespoon minced onion browned in butter; 1 tablespoon sherry (optional)
Creamy Cheese for vegetables or chicken	Cream of celery	Blend 3-ounce package of softened cream cheese with soup before adding ¼ to ⅓ cup milk
Curry for chicken, veal, lamb, or seafood	Cream of asparagus, celery, or chicken	¼ cup milk and ¼ to 1 teaspoon curry powder
Herb for chicken, fish, veal, vegetables, eggs	Cream of celery, chicken, or mushroom	¼ cup milk and dash of basil, marjoram, poultry seasoning, sage, or thyme
Nut for chicken, veal, or vegetables	Cream of mushroom	¼ cup milk and ¼ cup chopped walnuts or other nuts
Parsley for fish, eggs, vegetables	Cream of celery	¼ cup milk and 1 tablespoon chopped parsley
Pimiento-Egg for fish	Cream of celery	¼ cup milk, 1 tablespoon chopped onion browned in butter, 1 hard-cooked egg (chopped), 2 tablespoons chopped pimiento
Poulette for chicken or fish	Cream of chicken	¼ cup milk and 2 tablespoons minced onion browned in butter, 2 tablespoons chopped parsley, 2 teaspoons lemon juice, and 1 to 2 tablespoons sherry (optional)
Sour Cream for beef, chicken, fish	Cream of mushroom	¼ cup milk, 2 tablespoons chopped onion browned in butter, ¼ cup sour cream, ⅛ teaspoon paprika

TOMATO SOUP SAUCE

Plain Sauce: In saucepan, heat tomato soup just as it comes from the can. You may want to thin it a bit by adding a little water. Season as you like—with prepared mustard or horseradish, Worcestershire, hot pepper sauce, lemon juice, or herb such as thyme or oregano. 1 cup sauce. Use as a pour-on for: Pork chops, beef patties, corned beef hash, frankfurters, or fish sticks.

Tomato Horseradish Sauce: Stir in 2 tablespoons prepared horseradish, 1 tablespoon prepared mustard, dash of ground cloves, and pepper. 1 cup sauce. Serve with beef, ham, frankfurters, or meat loaf.

Tomato Cheese Sauce: Add ⅓ cup milk and ½ cup shredded Cheddar cheese. Heat; stir often until cheese is melted. 1½ cups sauce. Serve with fish, omelet, or vegetables.

EGG CHEESE SAUCE

1 can (11 ounces) condensed
  Cheddar cheese soup
¼ cup milk
1 hard-cooked egg, sliced
¼ teaspoon prepared mustard

In saucepan, stir soup until smooth. Gradually blend in milk; add egg and mustard. Heat; stir often. 1½ cups sauce. Serve over cooked broccoli or cauliflower.

SAUCE CREVETTES

1 tablespoon chopped green onion
Dash crushed thyme leaves
1 tablespoon butter or margarine
1 can (10¾ ounces) condensed
  cream of mushroom soup
½ cup milk
1 cup diced cooked shrimp
1 tablespoon chopped ripe olives

In saucepan, cook onion with thyme in butter until onion is tender. Add remaining ingredients. Heat; stir occasionally. Serve over poached eggs on toast. Makes 2 cups sauce.

CREAMY TOMATO SAUCE

¼ cup chopped onion
⅛ teaspoon thyme leaves, crushed
1 tablespoon butter or margarine
1 can (10¾ ounces) condensed
   tomato soup
½ cup sour cream
¼ cup water
2 teaspoons paprika

In saucepan, cook onion with thyme in butter until tender. Blend in remaining ingredients. Heat; stir occasionally. Makes about 2 cups.

CUCUMBER SAUCE

2 tablespoons chopped onion
2 tablespoons butter or margarine
1 can (10¾ ounces) condensed
   cream of celery soup
⅓ cup milk
¼ cup chopped cucumber
1 teaspoon lemon juice

In saucepan, cook onion in butter until tender. Add remaining ingredients. Heat; stir occasionally. Makes about 2 cups. Serve over cooked shrimp or white fish.

HERB-CHEESE SAUCE

1 can (10¾ ounces) condensed
   cream of mushroom soup
⅓ to ½ cup milk
1 cup shredded Cheddar cheese
1 tablespoon chopped parsley
Generous dash tarragon, crushed

In saucepan, stir soup until smooth; blend in milk. Add remaining ingredients. Heat; stir often. 2 cups sauce. Serve over cooked peas and onions, green beans, or broccoli.

STROGANOFF SAUCE

¼ cup chopped onion
2 tablespoons butter or margarine
1 can (10¾ ounces) condensed
   golden mushroom soup
¼ cup sour cream
½ teaspoon paprika

In saucepan, cook onion in butter until tender. Stir in remaining ingredients. Heat; stir occasionally. Makes 1½ cups sauce. Serve with beef patties or sliced cooked beef or veal.

SPAGHETTI WITH CLAM-OYSTER SAUCE

2 cans (about 8 ounces each)
  minced clams
2 tablespoons flour
½ cup chopped onion
¼ cup chopped parsley
1 medium clove garlic, minced
¼ cup olive oil
1 can (10½ ounces) condensed
  oyster stew
1 teaspoon lemon juice
Cooked spaghetti
Grated Parmesan cheese

Drain clams, reserving juice. Gradually blend clam juice into flour until smooth. In saucepan, cook onion with parsley and garlic in oil until tender. Add stew, clams, lemon juice, and flour mixture. Cook, stirring until thickened. Serve over spaghetti with cheese. Makes about 2 cups.

WHITE CLAM SAUCE

1 can (about 8 ounces) minced
  clams
2 medium cloves garlic, minced
2 tablespoons chopped parsley
2 tablespoons butter or margarine
1 can (10¾ ounces) condensed
  cream of mushroom soup
¼ cup milk
1 to 2 tablespoons grated
  Parmesan cheese
Cooked spaghetti

Drain clams, reserving juice. In saucepan, cook clams, garlic, and parsley in butter a few minutes. Stir in soup, milk, clam juice, and cheese. Cook over low heat 10 minutes. Stir occasionally. Serve over spaghetti. Makes about 2 cups.

CELERY-CAPER SAUCE FOR COLD MEAT

1 can (10¾ ounces) condensed
   cream of celery soup
¼ cup mayonnaise
1 tablespoon capers

Place unopened can of soup in refrigerator 3 to 4 hours. Blend soup and mayonnaise; stir in capers. Serve with cold cooked salmon, sliced beef, or ham. 1½ cups sauce.

VARIATIONS:

Dill Sauce: Substitute 1 teaspoon lemon juice and ½ teaspoon dried dill leaves for capers. Serve with cold cooked salmon. 1½ cups sauce.

Horseradish Sauce: Substitute 1 to 2 teaspoons horseradish for capers. Serve with cold sliced beef or ham. 1½ cups sauce.

Mustard Sauce: Substitute 1 teaspoon mustard for capers. Serve with cold sliced beef or ham. 1½ cups sauce.

SAUCE A L'ORANGE

1 tablespoon chopped onion
2 tablespoons butter, margarine, or
   drippings
1 can (10¾ ounces) condensed
   cream of mushroom soup
⅓ cup orange juice
1 teaspoon grated orange rind
⅛ teaspoon ground ginger

In saucepan, cook onion in butter until tender. Blend in remaining ingredients; stir until smooth. Heat. 1½ cups sauce. Especially good with roast duck.

TOMATO TOPPER FOR EGGS

¼ pound link sausage, thinly sliced
¼ cup chopped onion
2 tablespoons chopped green
   pepper
1 can (11 ounces) condensed
   tomato rice soup
½ cup water
1 tablespoon dry red wine

In saucepan, cook sausage, onion, and green pepper until done; pour off fat. Blend in soup, water, and wine. Heat; stir occasionally. Makes about 2 cups. Serve over omelet or scrambled eggs.

ALMOND-CHEESE SAUCE

1 can (11 ounces) condensed
   Cheddar cheese soup
¼ cup milk
¼ cup slivered almonds
¼ teaspoon curry powder

In saucepan, stir soup until smooth. Gradually blend in milk; add remaining ingredients. Heat; stir often. 1½ cups sauce. Serve over cooked broccoli or cauliflower.

QUICK TOULONNAISE SAUCE

2 tablespoons sliced green onion
1 tablespoon butter or margarine
1 can (10¾ ounces) condensed
   cream of celery soup
⅓ cup milk
2 tablespoons Chablis or other
   dry white wine
1 tablespoon capers
1 tablespoon chopped ripe olives

In saucepan, cook onion in butter until tender; add remaining ingredients. Heat; stir occasionally. Makes 1½ cups sauce. Serve over asparagus.

TANGY FISH SAUCE

¼ cup chopped celery
1 small clove garlic, minced
⅛ teaspoon dry mustard
2 tablespoons butter or margarine
1 can (11 ounces) condensed
   Cheddar cheese soup
⅓ cup milk
1 tablespoon chopped dill pickle

In saucepan, cook celery with garlic and mustard in butter until tender. Add remaining ingredients. Heat; stir occasionally. Makes about 1½ cups. Serve over cooked white fish.

MOCK HOLLANDAISE

1 can (10¾ ounces) condensed
   cream of celery, chicken, or
   mushroom soup
½ cup milk
2 tablespoons butter or margarine
2 tablespoons lemon juice
2 egg yolks, slightly beaten

In saucepan, combine all ingredients. Cook over low heat just until thickened, stirring constantly. *Do not boil.* 1½ cups sauce. Serve with cooked vegetables or fish.

EASY HOLLANDAISE: Use any cream soup. Omit milk, butter, and egg yolks. Reduce lemon juice to 1 tablespoon and add ¼ cup mayonnaise.

SAUCE CREOLE

1 small green pepper, sliced
1 small onion, sliced
1 can (4 ounces) sliced mushrooms,
   drained
2 tablespoons butter or margarine
1 can (10¾ ounces) condensed
   tomato soup
¼ cup water
1 teaspoon vinegar

In saucepan, cook green pepper, onion, and mushrooms in butter until tender. Stir in remaining ingredients. Cook over low heat 5 minutes. Stir occasionally. 2 cups sauce. Serve over omelet, hamburgers, or baked fish.

SOUPER GRAVY

1 can (10¾ ounces) condensed
   cream of celery, chicken, mushroom or golden mushroom soup
¼ cup milk or water
2 to 4 tablespoons drippings or
   butter

When preparing gravy for roast or fried meat, remove meat from pan and pour off and measure drippings. Pour can of soup into pan; stir well to loosen browned bits. Blend in water and drippings for thickness desired. Heat; stir often. 1½ cups gravy. Serve with fried chicken, roast beef, roast pork, pork chops, hamburgers, or baked ham.

QUICK ONION GRAVY

½ cup chopped onion
1 small clove garlic, minced
2 tablespoons butter or margarine
1 can (10¾ ounces) condensed
   golden mushroom soup
⅓ cup water
1 small bay leaf

In saucepan, cook onion with garlic in butter until tender. Stir in soup, water, and bay. Simmer a few minutes to blend flavors. Stir occasionally. Remove bay. Makes about 1½ cups.

CREAMY GIBLET GRAVY

½ cup chopped celery
2 tablespoons butter or margarine
1 can (10¾ ounces) condensed
   cream of chicken soup
⅓ cup water
½ cup chopped cooked giblets

In saucepan, cook celery in butter until tender. Blend in soup, water, and giblets. Heat; stir occasionally. Makes about 2 cups.

Barbecue Bonanza

Catch a whiff of meat or poultry barbecuing . . . that's the call to good eating. Barbecues can be held outside on the grill, or inside—on a rotisserie, in the oven, on an hibachi in the fireplace, or even in a skillet on top of the range. Whatever the location, it's smart to reach for the soup can when sauce-making time arrives. The results are guaranteed to be great.

An easy reputation as a barbecue chef is yours when you choose a good long-handled pastry brush, a cut of meat which turns crisp and luscious over carefully controlled heat, and one of the following sauces. Bring on the feast!

ALL 'ROUND TOMATO BARBECUE SAUCE

1 can (10¾ ounces) condensed tomato soup
2 to 4 tablespoons sweet pickle relish
¼ cup finely chopped onion
1 tablespoon brown sugar
1 tablespoon vinegar
1 tablespoon Worcestershire

In saucepan, combine all ingredients. Cover; cook over low heat 10 minutes. Stir occasionally. Makes about 1½ cups.

BARBECUED FRANKFURTERS

SKILLET: Combine sauce as directed. Add 1 pound frankfurters. Cover; cook over low heat 10 minutes. Stir often. 4 servings.

OUTDOOR COOKING: Prepare sauce as directed. Slit 2 pounds frankfurters lengthwise; brush with sauce. Place on grill over glowing coals. Cook, brushing with sauce and turning every few minutes, until nicely browned. 8 servings.

BARBECUED HAMBURGERS

SKILLET: Shape 2 pounds seasoned ground beef into 8 patties. In skillet, brown patties (use shortening if necessary); pour off fat. Add sauce ingredients. Cook over low heat 20 minutes or until done. 8 servings

OUTDOOR COOKING: Prepare sauce as directed. Make patties as in skillet method. Place on grill about 6 inches above glowing coals. Cook about 15 minutes, brushing with sauce and turning every 5 minutes. 8 servings.

BARBECUED CHICKEN

SKILLET: Brown 2 pounds chicken parts in 2 to 4 tablespoons butter or margarine. Add sauce ingredients. Cover; simmer 45 minutes or until chicken is done. Stir occasionally. 4 to 6 servings.

OUTDOOR COOKING: Prepare sauce. Brush 2 split broilers (2½ pounds each) with salad oil; place on grill, skin-side up, about 6 inches above glowing coals. Cook 15 minutes on each side. Brush with sauce; cook 30 minutes more or until chicken is tender, turning and brushing with sauce every 5 minutes. 4 servings.

BARBECUED STEAK

OUTDOOR COOKING: Prepare sauce. Place 2 pounds sirloin steak (about 1" thick) on grill about 4 inches above glowing coals. Brush with sauce; cook 5 minutes. Turn; brush with sauce. Cook 5 minutes longer or until desired doneness. Heat remaining sauce. Serve with steak. 4 servings.

ZESTY BARBECUE SAUCE

⅓ cup chopped green onion
1 tablespoon chopped hot cherry
  peppers
2 tablespoons butter or margarine
1 can (10¾ ounces) condensed
  tomato soup
¼ cup water
1 tablespoon brown sugar
1 teaspoon prepared horseradish

In saucepan, cook onion and peppers in butter until onion is tender. Add remaining ingredients. Simmer 15 minutes or until flavors are blended; stir often. 1½ cups sauce.

FRANK SANDWICHES

Prepare sauce. Slit 1 pound frankfurters lengthwise. Place on broiler pan; brush with sauce. Broil about 4 inches from heat until done, brushing with sauce and turning often. Serve on toasted buns. 4 servings.

BURGER SANDWICHES

Prepare sauce. Shape 1½ pounds seasoned ground beef into 6 patties. Place on broiler pan; brush with sauce. Broil about 4 inches from heat until done, brushing with sauce and turning often. Serve on toasted buns. 6 servings.

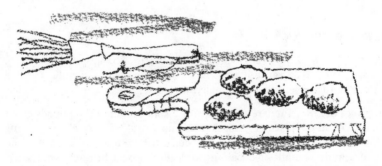

SPEEDY BARBECUE SAUCE

¼ cup chopped celery
1 teaspoon chili powder
2 tablespoons salad oil
1 can (10½ ounces) condensed
  onion soup
1 tablespoon cornstarch
½ cup ketchup
¼ cup water
1 tablespoon vinegar
1 teaspoon prepared mustard

In saucepan, cook celery with chili powder in oil until tender; add remaining ingredients. Cook over low heat 10 minutes; stir occasionally. Makes about 2 cups. Use as a basting sauce for hamburgers, frankfurters, chicken, or spareribs. Serve with remaining sauce.

ONION BARBECUE SAUCE

1 can (10¾ ounces) condensed
  cream of mushroom soup
1 can (10½ ounces) condensed
  onion soup
½ cup ketchup
¼ cup salad oil
¼ cup vinegar
2 large cloves garlic, minced
2 tablespoons brown sugar
1 tablespoon Worcestershire
⅛ teaspoon hot pepper sauce

In saucepan, combine all ingredients. Cover; simmer 15 minutes; stir often. 3 cups sauce.

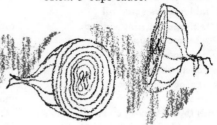

OUTDOOR CHICKEN

Prepare sauce. Brush 4 split broilers with salad oil. Place on grill (skin-side up) about 6 inches above glowing coals. Cook 15 minutes; turn; cook 15 minutes more. Brush with sauce; continue cooking 30 minutes or until chicken is done, brushing with sauce and turning every 5 minutes. 8 servings.

OUTDOOR SPARERIBS

Place 6 pounds spareribs (cut into serving-size pieces) in a large pot of boiling water. Cover; simmer 1 hour; drain. Prepare sauce as directed. Place ribs on grill about 6 inches above glowing coals. Brush with sauce; continue cooking 30 minutes or until done, brushing with sauce and turning every 5 minutes. 6 servings.

OVEN BARBECUED SPARERIBS

4 pounds spareribs, cut in
  serving-size pieces
1 can (10½ ounces) condensed
  beef broth
1 cup prepared mincemeat
3 tablespoons vinegar
2 tablespoons cornstarch

In large heavy pan, cover ribs with water. Simmer 1 hour; drain and cool. Arrange in roasting pan (13x 9x2"). Meanwhile, in saucepan, combine remaining ingredients. Heat, stirring until thickened. Pour sauce over ribs. Bake at 450°F. for 30 minutes or until done. Makes 4 servings.

BARBECUED LAMB KABOBS

1 can (10¾ ounces) condensed
   tomato soup
1 small clove garlic, minced
2 tablespoons salad oil
2 tablespoons wine vinegar
1 tablespoon sugar
½ teaspoon salt
⅛ teaspoon pepper
⅛ teaspoon oregano leaves,
   crushed
Dash thyme leaves, crushed
1 pound lamb cubes for kabobs
   (1½-inch)
1 medium green pepper,
   cut in 1½-inch pieces
1 can (16 ounces) small whole
   white onions, drained

Combine soup, garlic, oil, vinegar, sugar, and seasonings; add lamb. Refrigerate 4 hours or more. On 2 skewers, arrange green pepper and onions. On 4 separate skewers, arrange lamb; place lamb kabobs on broiler pan. Broil 4 inches from heat for 15 minutes or until desired doneness, turning and brushing with marinade. Brush vegetable kabobs with marinade; broil 10 minutes. Heat remaining marinade; serve with kabobs. Makes 4 servings.
OUTDOOR METHOD: Marinate kabobs as above. Place on grill 4 inches above glowing coals. Cook 15 minutes or until desired doneness, turning and brushing with marinade. Brush vegetable kabobs with marinade; cook 10 minutes.

SKILLET BARBECUED CHICKEN

2 pounds chicken parts
½ teaspoon salt
Dash pepper
¼ cup butter or margarine
1 can (10¾ ounces) condensed
   tomato soup
½ cup chopped onion
3 tablespoons wine vinegar
2 tablespoons brown sugar
1 tablespoon Worcestershire
Dash sweet basil
Dash leaf thyme
Generous dash hot pepper sauce

Season chicken with salt and pepper. In skillet, brown chicken in butter. Stir in remaining ingredients. Cover. Cook over low heat 45 minutes or until chicken is tender; stir occasionally. Makes 4 servings.

Vegetables with New Flavor

Maybe vegetables are your idea of heaven. Then again, maybe they're not. Either way, these recipes are for you. Each one opens up new vistas of vegetable flavor for both the aficionado and the indifferent.

Dish up a casserole of green beans baked to creamy perfection. Add unexpected tang and color to baked potatoes. Soup makes the difference.

A word about vegetable cookery: if vegetables could talk, they'd surely advise, "don't overcook. We're best *just* tender." And to save nutrients, handle with care, cook with the least amount of water, simmer gently.

VEGETABLE-CHEESE BAKE

1 large bunch broccoli or head
  cauliflower (or two 10-ounce
  packages frozen), cooked
  and drained
1 can (10¾ ounces) condensed
  cream of celery, chicken, or
  mushroom soup
⅓ to ½ cup milk
½ cup shredded sharp Cheddar
  cheese
¼ cup buttered bread crumbs

Place broccoli or cauliflower in shallow baking dish (10x6x2"). Blend soup, milk, and cheese; pour over vegetable. Top with crumbs. Bake in a 350°F. oven 30 minutes or until bubbling. 6 servings.

EASY CREAMED VEGETABLES

Top-of-stove method: Cook 2 packages (10 ounces each) frozen vegetables (cauliflower, corn, green beans, lima beans, mixed vegetables, peas, peas and carrots, spinach) in unsalted water until tender; drain. Stir in 1 can condensed cream of celery, chicken, mushroom, or Cheddar cheese soup; heat. Thin to desired consistency with milk. Season to taste. 6 servings.

SAVORY POTATOES

2 slices bacon
½ cup chopped onion
1 can (10¾ ounces) condensed cream of mushroom soup
Dash pepper
⅓ cup milk
5 cups cubed cooked potatoes

In saucepan, cook bacon until crisp; remove and crumble. Pour off all but 2 tablespoons drippings. Cook onion in drippings until tender. Stir in soup and pepper; gradually blend in milk. Add potatoes. Heat; stir occasionally. Garnish with bacon. Makes about 5 cups.

SCALLOPED POTATOES

1 can (11 ounces) condensed Cheddar cheese, cream of celery, chicken, or mushroom soup
½ cup milk
Dash pepper
4 cups thinly sliced potatoes
1 small onion, thinly sliced
1 tablespoon butter or margarine
Dash paprika

Blend soup, milk, and pepper. In buttered 1½-quart casserole, arrange alternate layers of potatoes, onion, and sauce. Dot top with butter; sprinkle with paprika. Cover; bake in a 375° oven 1 hour. Uncover; bake 15 minutes more. Makes about 3½ cups. NOTE: Sliced cooked potatoes may be substituted for raw potatoes. Mince onion and reduce cooking time to about 30 minutes; bake uncovered.

CHINESE VEGETABLES

2 cups diagonally sliced celery
1 cup diagonally sliced green onion
2 tablespoons salad oil
1 can (10¾ ounces) condensed chicken broth
½ cup water
1 can (16 ounces) Chinese vegetables, drained
3 tablespoons cornstarch
2 tablespoons soy sauce
Cooked rice

In skillet, cook celery and onion in oil until *just* tender. Add remaining ingredients except rice. Cook, stirring until thickened. Serve over rice with additional soy. Makes about 3½ cups.

Instant Cheese Sauce   Page 52

CREAMED ONIONS AND PEAS

1 can (10¾ ounces) condensed
cream of mushroom soup
⅓ cup milk
1 package (10 ounces) frozen peas,
cooked and drained
1 can (16 ounces) small whole
white onions, drained
Dash pepper

In saucepan, blend soup and milk; add remaining ingredients. Heat; stir occasionally. Makes about 3½ cups.

GOLDEN VEGETABLE COMBO

¼ cup chopped onion
Generous dash crushed thyme
2 tablespoons butter or margarine
1 can (11 ounces) condensed
Cheddar cheese soup
1 package (10 ounces) frozen
Brussels sprouts, cooked and
drained
1 package (10 ounces) frozen
cauliflower, cooked and drained
⅓ cup drained chopped canned
tomatoes

In saucepan, cook onion with thyme in butter until tender. Add remaining ingredients. Heat; stir occasionally. Makes about 4 cups.

GREEN BEANS ITALIANO

4 slices bacon
1 cup sliced onion
2 medium cloves garlic, minced
1 teaspoon oregano leaves, crushed
¼ teaspoon basil leaves, crushed
1 can (10¾ ounces) condensed
tomato soup
¼ cup water
2 packages (9 ounces each) frozen
cut green beans
Grated Parmesan cheese

In skillet, cook bacon until crisp; remove and crumble. Pour off all but 2 tablespoons drippings. Cook onion with garlic, oregano, and basil in drippings until tender. Add soup, water, and beans. Cover; cook over low heat 20 minutes or until beans are tender. Stir occasionally. Garnish with bacon and cheese. Makes about 3½ cups.

Arroz Con Pollo   Page 99

ZESTY BUTTER BEANS

¼ cup chopped green pepper
¼ cup chopped onion
2 tablespoons butter or margarine
1 can (10¾ ounces) condensed
  tomato soup
¼ cup water
2 cans (16 ounces each) butter
  beans, drained
1 can (16 ounces) cut green beans,
  drained
1 tablespoon brown sugar
1 tablespoon vinegar
1 teaspoon prepared mustard

In saucepan, cook green pepper and onion in butter until tender. Add remaining ingredients. Simmer a few minutes to blend flavors. Stir occasionally. Makes about 5 cups.

CALICO CORN

4 slices bacon
¼ cup green pepper strips
1 can (11 ounces) condensed
  Cheddar cheese soup
3 cups cooked whole kernel corn
½ cup drained chopped canned
  tomatoes

In saucepan, cook bacon until crisp; remove and crumble. Pour off all but 2 tablespoons drippings. Cook green pepper in drippings until tender. Add soup, corn, and tomatoes. Heat; stir occasionally. Garnish with bacon. Makes about 4 cups.

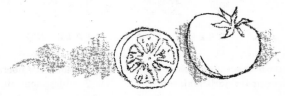

SUMMERTIME FRIED TOMATOES

4 medium tomatoes, sliced
⅓ cup seasoned flour
¼ cup butter or margarine
1 can (10¾ ounces) condensed
  cream of mushroom soup
⅓ cup milk

Dip tomato slices in seasoned flour. Cook in butter over low heat until lightly browned on both sides. Remove to heated platter. Stir soup and milk into skillet. Heat; stir occasionally. Pour sauce over tomatoes. 4 to 6 servings.

CREAMED MEDLEY

1 package (10 ounces) frozen
  sliced carrots
1 package (10 ounces) frozen
  cauliflower
1 package (10 ounces) frozen
  green peas
1 can (10¾ ounces) condensed
  cream of chicken soup
¼ cup chopped parsley
1 tablespoon instant minced onion
½ teaspoon salt
1 cup shredded sharp Cheddar
  cheese

Thaw vegetables just enough to separate. In bowl, blend soup, parsley, onion, and salt. Mix in vegetables. Pour into 1½-quart casserole. Bake at 400°F. for 35 minutes or until done; stir. Top with cheese. Bake until cheese melts. Makes about 4½ cups.

ITALIAN EGGPLANT BAKE

1 medium eggplant (about 1
  pound), peeled and cut in
  1½-inch pieces
1 large onion, sliced
1 medium green pepper,
  cut in strips
1 small clove garlic, minced
1 teaspoon oregano leaves, crushed
4 tablespoons butter or margarine
1 can (10¾ ounces) condensed
  tomato soup
1 cup water
¼ teaspoon salt
1 cup garlic croutons
¼ cup grated Parmesan cheese

Cook eggplant in boiling salted water for 3 minutes; drain. In saucepan, cook onion and green pepper with garlic and oregano in butter until tender. Add soup, water, eggplant, and salt. Pour into shallow baking dish (10x6x2"). Bake at 350°F. for 35 minutes or until hot; stir. Top with croutons; sprinkle with cheese. Bake 5 minutes more. Makes about 5 cups.

GREEN BEAN CASSEROLE

1 can (10¾ ounces) condensed
  cream of chicken or mushroom
  soup
⅓ cup milk
1 teaspoon soy sauce
Dash pepper
3 cups cooked French style green
  beans (or two 10-ounce packages
  frozen, or two 1-pound cans),
  drained
1 can (3½ ounces) French fried
  onions

In 1½-quart casserole, stir soup, milk, soy sauce, and pepper until smooth; mix in beans and ½ can onions. Bake at 350°F. for 25 minutes or until hot. Stir. Top with remaining onions. Bake 5 minutes more. Makes about 4 cups.

Egg and Cheese Cookery

Make way for the meatless wonders: eggs and cheese. In main dishes they're unsurpassed—proteinwise, tastewise, and pennywise. Teamed with soup, they're extraordinary.

Soup sauces enrich egg dishes, flavor up cheese fondues and casseroles. When it comes to souffles, soup really shows off. You can make this dramatic dish with any of five kinds of soup. Need an easygoing cheese sauce? See the Saucery section.

Remember, both eggs and cheese are delicate, so avoid cooking them at high temperatures.

EGG CROQUETTES

1 can (10¾ ounces) condensed
    cream of celery soup
8 hard-cooked eggs, finely chopped
¼ cup fine dry bread crumbs
2 tablespoons finely chopped onion
2 tablespoons finely chopped
    parsley
½ teaspoon salt
Dash pepper
Shortening
⅓ to ½ cup milk

Combine 2 tablespoons soup, eggs, bread crumbs, onion, parsley, salt, and pepper. Mix well; shape into 8 croquettes or patties. (If mixture is difficult to handle, chill before shaping.) Roll in additional bread crumbs. In skillet, brown croquettes in shortening. Meanwhile, in saucepan, combine remaining soup and milk. Heat; stir occasionally. Serve with croquettes. Makes 4 servings.

EASY CHEESE SOUFFLÉ

1 can (11 ounces) condensed
Cheddar cheese soup
6 eggs, separated

In saucepan, heat soup, stirring; remove from heat. Beat egg yolks until thick and lemon-colored; stir into soup. In large bowl, using clean egg beater, beat egg whites until stiff; fold soup mixture into egg whites. Pour into 1½-quart casserole. Bake at 300°F. for 1 to 1¼ hours or at 400°F. for 30 minutes. Serve immediately. 4 servings.

SOUPER CHEESE SOUFFLÉ

1 can (10¾ ounces) condensed
cream of celery, chicken,
mushroom, or shrimp soup
1 cup shredded sharp process
cheese
6 eggs, separated

In saucepan, combine soup and cheese; heat slowly until cheese melts. Remove from heat. Beat egg yolks until thick and lemon-colored; stir into soup mixture. Beat egg whites until stiff; fold soup mixture into egg whites. Pour into ungreased 1½-quart casserole. Bake at 300°F. 1 to 1¼ hours or at 400°F. 30 minutes. Serve immediately. 4 servings.

Try these additions to vary the basic souffle; bake in a 2-quart casserole:

Shrimp Surprise Soufflé: ½ cup finely chopped cooked broccoli, well-drained, ¼ teaspoon lemon juice, and a dash ground nutmeg to cream of shrimp soup-cheese mixture. Proceed as above.

Asparagus Soufflé: ⅛ teaspoon ground nutmeg and ½ cup finely chopped cooked asparagus to cream of mushroom soup-cheese mixture. Proceed as above.

Ham-Mushroom Soufflé: ¼ teaspoon chervil, ½ cup finely minced cooked ham, and 2 tablespoons chopped parsley to cream of mushroom soup-cheese mixture. Proceed as above.

RUM TUM DITTY

1 can (10¾ ounces) condensed
tomato soup
¼ cup water
1 cup shredded sharp Cheddar
cheese
Toast

In saucepan, combine soup, water, and cheese. Cook over low heat; stir often until cheese is melted. Serve over toast. If desired, garnish with hard-cooked egg slices or sardines. Makes about 1½ cups.

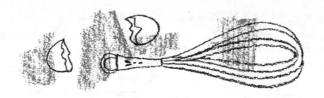

EASY EGGS BENEDICT

1 can (10¾ ounces) condensed
   cream of celery, chicken, or
   mushroom soup
⅓ cup milk
6 thin slices ham, fried
6 slices buttered toast or English
   muffin halves
6 eggs, poached
1 tablespoon minced parsley

In saucepan, blend soup and milk. Heat; stir occasionally. Meanwhile, place a slice of ham on each slice of toast or muffin half; top with poached egg. Pour sauce over eggs. Sprinkle with minced parsley. 6 servings.

SHRIMP OMELET

SAUCE:
1 can (10¾ ounces) condensed
   cream of mushroom soup
1 cup diced cooked shrimp
⅓ cup milk
2 tablespoons chopped parsley

OMELET:
8 eggs
½ cup milk
¼ teaspoon salt
Dash pepper
4 tablespoons butter or margarine

To make sauce, in saucepan, combine soup, shrimp, milk, and parsley. Heat; stir occasionally. To make omelet, beat eggs, milk, salt, and pepper. In skillet, melt butter; pour in egg mixture. Cook slowly. As undersurface becomes set, lift slightly to allow uncooked egg to flow underneath and cook. When omelet is done, transfer to platter. Make a shallow cut down the center; pour part of sauce on half of the omelet; fold over. Serve with remaining sauce. 4 servings.

STRACCIATELLE

1 can (10¾ ounces) condensed
   chicken broth
1 soup can water
1 egg
2 tablespoons grated Parmesan
   cheese
1 tablespoon chopped parsley

In saucepan, combine chicken broth and water; bring to boil. Beat egg with cheese and parsley; gradually pour into simmering soup, stirring gently until egg is set. Serve immediately. Makes about 3 cups.

CREAMED EGGS

1 can (10¾ ounces) condensed
   cream of celery soup
⅓ to ½ cup milk
6 hard-cooked eggs, sliced
2 tablespoons chopped pimiento
Toast

In saucepan, blend soup and milk. Add eggs and pimiento. Heat; stir occasionally. Serve on toast. Makes about 3 cups.

Eggs Goldenrod: Omit pimiento. Separate cooked egg yolks and whites; chop whites coarsely; force yolks through a fine sieve. Add egg whites to sauce. Garnish with sieved yolks.

BAKED CHEESE FONDUE

3 eggs, separated
1 can (10¾ ounces) condensed
   cream of celery, chicken, or
   mushroom soup
2 cups small bread cubes
1 cup shredded sharp Cheddar or
   process cheese
¼ teaspoon dry mustard

Beat egg whites until stiff but not dry; beat yolks until thick. Combine yolks, soup, bread, cheese, and mustard; gently fold in whites. Pour into 1½ -quart casserole. Bake at 325°F. for 1 hour. 4 servings.

SWISS FONDUE

1 large clove garlic, cut in half
1 cup Chablis or other dry
   white wine
1 can (11 ounces) condensed
   Cheddar cheese soup
1 pound natural Swiss cheese,
   cubed or shredded
3 tablespoons cornstarch
French or Italian bread cubes

Rub inside of fondue pot or saucepan with cut edge of garlic, then discard. In fondue pot, simmer wine. Blend in soup. Combine cheese and cornstarch; stir into soup mixture. Heat until cheese melts; stir occasionally. Spear bread with fondue fork and dip into fondue. Makes about 4 cups.

EGG AND OYSTERS AU GRATIN

1 can (10½ ounces) condensed
  oyster stew
¼ cup milk
2 tablespoons flour
½ cup shredded sharp Cheddar
  cheese
6 hard-cooked eggs, sliced
Cooked asparagus or broccoli spears

Empty stew into saucepan. Gradually blend milk into flour until smooth; slowly stir into stew. Add cheese. Cook, stirring until thickened and cheese is melted. Add eggs; heat. Serve over asparagus; garnish with paprika. Makes about 2½ cups.

EGGS FLORENTINE

1 can (10¾ ounces) condensed
  cream of celery soup
¼ cup milk
2 packages (10 ounces each)
  frozen chopped spinach, cooked
  and well-drained
6 eggs
1 cup shredded mild process cheese

In 1½-quart shallow baking dish (10x6x2"), combine soup, milk, and spinach. Spread evenly in bottom of dish. Top mixture with eggs; sprinkle with cheese. Bake at 350°F. for 30 minutes or until eggs are set. Makes 6 servings.

QUICK EGG CURRY

1 can (10¾ ounces) condensed
  cream of mushroom soup
⅓ cup milk
1 teaspoon curry powder
4 hard-cooked eggs, sliced
4 slices bread, toasted
Shredded coconut, toasted slivered
  almonds, chutney, or raisins

In saucepan, stir soup until smooth. Blend in milk and curry powder. Heat; stir often. Add eggs. Serve over toast with coconut, almonds, chutney, or raisins. Makes about 2½ cups.

WESTERN SCRAMBLE

½ cup chopped cooked ham
¼ cup chopped green pepper
¼ cup chopped onion
4 tablespoons butter or margarine
1 can (11 ounces) condensed
  Cheddar cheese soup
8 eggs, slightly beaten

In 10-inch skillet, brown ham and cook green pepper and onion in butter until tender. Meanwhile, in bowl, stir soup until smooth; gradually blend in eggs. Add to ham mixture. Cook over low heat. As mixture begins to set around edges, gently lift cooked portions with large turner so that thin uncooked portion can flow to the bottom. Continue gently lifting cooked portions until eggs are completely set, but still moist. 4 servings.

EGGS IN CHEESE SAUCE

1 can (10¾ ounces) condensed
   cream of celery or mushroom soup
⅓ to ½ cup milk
½ cup shredded sharp Cheddar
   cheese
4 hard-cooked eggs, sliced
4 slices toast
Chopped parsley, if desired

In saucepan, combine soup, milk, and cheese. Cook over low heat until cheese melts. Stir often. Add eggs. Serve on toast, rice, or asparagus. Garnish with parsley. Makes about 3 cups.

CURRIED EGGS

6 hard-cooked eggs
¼ cup mayonnaise
¼ teaspoon curry powder
1 can (10¾ ounces) condensed
   cream of mushroom soup
½ cup milk
Toast or English muffins, split
   and toasted
Paprika

Cut eggs in half lengthwise. Carefully remove egg yolks. In small bowl, mash yolks with fork. Blend in mayonnaise and curry powder. Stuff into egg whites. In skillet, combine soup and milk. Arrange eggs filled side up in sauce. Cover; cook over low heat 5 minutes or until eggs are hot. Serve eggs on toast; spoon sauce over all. Sprinkle with paprika. 3 servings.

GOLDEN RABBIT

1 can (11 ounces) condensed
   Cheddar cheese soup
1 can (10¾ ounces) condensed
   tomato soup
⅓ cup milk
Toast

In saucepan, blend soups and milk. Heat; stir often. Serve over toast. Makes about 2½ cups.

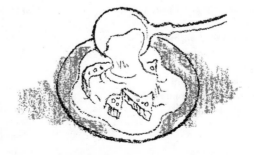

Salads and Salad Dressings

So you adore salads! Because they're light and refreshing anytime. Because they have a knack for adding that just-right splash of color to meals. Because they're nutritious.

Here are some new ones to brighten your repertoire—molded, tossed, hot. And dressings—smooth, spicy, imaginative. Even low calorie. Each is flavored with that handy ingredient, a can of condensed soup.

HAM AND MACARONI TOSS

1 can (10¾ ounces) condensed
  cream of chicken soup
¼ cup chopped celery
¼ cup chopped onion
2 tablespoons chopped green
  pepper
½ teaspoon prepared mustard
Dash hot pepper sauce
Dash pepper
2 cups cooked macaroni
1½ cups diced cooked ham
Tomatoes, cut in wedges

Combine soup, celery, onion, green pepper, mustard, hot pepper sauce, and pepper. Add macaroni and ham. Chill. Serve with tomato wedges. Makes about 4 cups.

TIP: To unmold gelatine salads, dip pan bottom briefly in warm (not hot) water. Run knife along edges to permit air to flow in. Tap sharply once or twice. Invert on moistened serving plate (this permits you to shift mold if necessary); raise pan and release salad.

SEASHORE SALAD

2 envelopes unflavored gelatine
2 cups cold water
1 can (10¾ ounces) condensed tomato soup
1 tablespoon lemon juice
1 package (8 ounces) cream cheese, softened
1 cup diced cooked shrimp
½ cup chopped celery
2 tablespoons chopped green onion

In saucepan, sprinkle gelatine on cold water to soften. Place over low heat, stirring until gelatine is dissolved. Remove from heat; gradually stir in soup and lemon juice. Stir cream cheese until smooth; gradually blend in gelatine mixture. Chill until slightly thickened. Fold in remaining ingredients. Pour into 1-quart mold. Chill until firm. Unmold and serve on crisp salad greens. Makes about 4 cups.

CREAMY TUNA MOLD

2 envelopes unflavored gelatine
2 cups cold water
1 can (10¾ ounces) condensed cream of celery soup
1 tablespoon lemon juice
1 package (3 ounces) cream cheese, softened
1 can (about 7 ounces) tuna, drained and flaked
½ cup shredded carrot
½ cup chopped celery
2 tablespoons chopped parsley

In saucepan, sprinkle gelatine on 1 cup cold water to soften. Place over low heat, stirring until gelatine is dissolved. Remove from heat. Blend soup and lemon juice into cream cheese; gradually blend in gelatine and remaining water. Chill until slightly thickened. Fold in remaining ingredients. Pour into 5-cup mold. Chill until firm. Unmold; serve on crisp salad greens. Makes about 4½ cups.

ROSY AND WHITE ASPIC

1 envelope unflavored gelatine
½ cup cold water
1 can (10¾ ounces) condensed tomato soup
1 teaspoon grated onion
Crisp salad greens
1 cup creamy cottage cheese

Sprinkle gelatine on cold water to soften. Place over low heat; stir until gelatine is dissolved. Remove from heat; combine with soup and onion. Pour into 1-quart or 4 individual molds that have been rinsed with cold water. Chill until firm. Unmold; serve on salad greens with a topping of cottage cheese. Makes about 4 cups.

DOUBLE DECKER CHICKEN MOLD

First layer:

1 envelope unflavored gelatine
½ cup cold water
1 can (10¾ ounces) condensed
  cream of chicken soup
¼ cup mayonnaise
1 tablespoon lemon juice
1 can (5 ounces) boned chicken,
  or 1 cup diced cooked chicken
¼ cup chopped celery
2 tablespoons chopped toasted
  almonds
1 tablespoon finely chopped onion
Dash pepper

First layer: Sprinkle gelatine on cold water to soften. Place over low heat; stir until gelatine is dissolved. Remove from heat. Blend soup, mayonnaise, and lemon juice; stir in gelatine. Chill until mixture begins to thicken. Fold in remaining ingredients. Pour into 1½-quart mold. Chill until almost firm.

Second layer:

1 envelope unflavored gelatine
½ cup cold water
1 can (1 pound) jellied cranberry
  sauce
1 orange, peeled and diced

Second layer: Sprinkle gelatine on cold water to soften. Place over low heat; stir until gelatine is dissolved. Remove from heat. Crush cranberry sauce with fork; add gelatine. Chill until mixture begins to thicken; fold in orange. Pour on top of chicken layer. Chill until firm. Unmold. Serve on crisp salad greens. Makes about 5 cups.

SPRINGTIME SALAD

1 can (10½ ounces) condensed
  beef broth
1 package (3 ounces) lemon-
  flavored gelatin
½ cup cold water
1 tablespoon grated onion
1 tablespoon vinegar
Dash salt
Dash pepper
1 cup diced cooked beef
⅓ cup diced red apple
2 tablespoons sliced celery

In saucepan, bring beef broth to a boil. Add gelatin; stir to dissolve. Add water, onion, vinegar, salt, and pepper. Chill until slightly thickened. Fold in remaining ingredients. Pour into a 3-cup mold. Chill until firm (about 4 hours). Makes about 2½ cups.

GERMAN POTATO SALAD

4 slices bacon
¾ cup chopped onion
1 can (10¾ ounces) condensed
   cream of celery or chicken soup
¼ cup water
2 to 3 tablespoons vinegar
½ teaspoon sugar
⅛ teaspoon pepper
4 cups sliced cooked potatoes
¼ cup chopped parsley

Cook bacon until crisp; remove from skillet; drain and crumble. Cook onion in bacon drippings until tender. Blend in soup, water, vinegar, sugar, and pepper. Heat; stir occasionally. Add potatoes, parsley, and bacon; simmer 5 minutes. Serve hot. Makes about 4 cups.

TOMATO FRENCH DRESSING

1 can (10¾ ounces) condensed
   tomato soup
¼ cup vinegar
½ cup salad oil
1 tablespoon minced onion
2 tablespoons sugar
2 teaspoons dry mustard
1 teaspoon salt
¼ teaspoon pepper

Combine all ingredients in jar. Shake well before using. Makes about 2 cups.

NOTE: To vary this TOMATO FRENCH DRESSING, add any one of the following:

Bacon Dressing—4 slices bacon, cooked and crumbled
Blue Cheese Dressing—¼ cup crumbled blue cheese
Chiffonade Dressing—1 chopped hard-cooked egg, 1 tablespoon minced green pepper, 1 tablespoon minced pimiento
Curry Dressing—½ teaspoon curry powder
Garlic Dressing—1 clove garlic, minced
Herb Dressing—1 teaspoon ground herb (marjoram, rosemary, sage, savory, or thyme)
Ripe Olive Dressing—¼ cup chopped ripe olives
Sweet Pickle Dressing—¼ cup sweet pickle relish
Vinaigrette Dressing—1 chopped hard-cooked egg and 1 tablespoon chopped parsley

RUSSIAN-STYLE DRESSING

1 can (10¾ ounces) condensed
   cream of celery soup
¼ cup mayonnaise
¼ cup chili sauce
1 teaspoon lemon juice
2 to 3 teaspoons minced onion,
   if desired

Place unopened can of soup in refrigerator 3 to 4 hours. Blend soup and mayonnaise; stir in remaining ingredients. Serve with asparagus or green salads. Makes about 1½ cups dressing.

QUICK GREEN GODDESS DRESSING

1 can (10¾ ounces) condensed
   cream of celery soup
¼ cup mayonnaise
2 tablespoons chopped parsley
4 anchovies, chopped
1 teaspoon lemon juice

Place unopened can of soup in refrigerator 3 to 4 hours. Blend soup and mayonnaise; stir in remaining ingredients. Serve with green salads. About 1½ cups dressing.

DRESSING LAMAZE

1 can (10¾ ounces) condensed
   tomato soup
1 cup mayonnaise
¼ cup India or sweet pickle relish
1 hard-cooked egg, chopped
½ teaspoon grated onion
½ teaspoon prepared mustard
1 tablespoon lemon juice

Blend soup and mayonnaise. Add remaining ingredients; mix well. Chill. Serve with cooked shrimp or green salads. About 2½ cups dressing.

LOW-CAL TOMATO DRESSING

1 can (10¾ ounces) condensed
   tomato soup
¼ cup water
2 tablespoons lemon juice
2 teaspoons grated onion
½ teaspoon prepared mustard
¼ teaspoon salt
Generous dash pepper

Combine all ingredients in a tightly covered container; shake until blended. Chill 4 hours. Makes about 1½ cups dressing.

DIETERS' DELIGHT

1 can (10½ ounces) condensed
   beef broth
2 tablespoons chili sauce
2 tablespoons vinegar
1 tablespoon grated onion

Combine all ingredients in a jar. Chill. Shake well before serving. Serve on crisp greens. Makes about 1 cup dressing.

Quick Breads and Pancakes

Looking for a new main dish idea? Something that's ready in a jiffy, yet pampers the whole family's taste, you say. Then follow this yummy formula:

Prepare a stack of pancakes or bake corn bread or biscuits from a mix. Combine diced chicken, ham, or seafood with a cream soup. Spoon the mixture over biscuits or pancakes. There. You have a dish to do you proud. For more along these delicious lines, try the following. Or bake this spunky spoonbread. Soup is the flavor-booster.

MINUTE TURKEY SHORTCAKE

1 can (10¾ ounces) condensed
  cream of chicken soup
½ cup milk
1½ cups diced cooked turkey
½ cup cooked peas
1 tablespoon chopped pimiento
Biscuits, corn bread, or pancakes

In saucepan, blend soup and milk. Combine remaining ingredients except biscuits. Heat; stir often. Serve over biscuits. Makes about 2½ cups.

SPOONBREAD

1 cup corn meal
1¼ cups water
3 tablespoons butter or margarine
1 can (11 ounces) condensed
  Cheddar cheese, cream of chicken,
  or mushroom soup
1 teaspoon baking powder
3 eggs, separated

In saucepan, combine corn meal and water; bring to a boil and cook until very thick, stirring constantly. Remove from heat and stir in butter. Add soup, baking powder, and slightly beaten egg yolks; mix well. Fold mixture into stiffly beaten egg whites. Pour into greased 2-quart casserole dish. Bake at 350°F. for 1 hour. Serve hot with butter and maple syrup if desired. 6 servings.

CREAMED CHICKEN WITH ALMONDS OVER PANCAKES

1 cup chopped celery
2 tablespoons butter or margarine
1 can (10¾ ounces) condensed
cream of chicken or
mushroom soup
⅓ to ½ cup milk
1 can (5 ounces) boned chicken, or
1 cup diced cooked chicken
2 tablespoons diced pimiento
¼ cup toasted slivered almonds
8 thin pancakes

In saucepan, cook celery in butter until tender; blend in soup and milk. Add chicken, pimiento, and almonds. Heat; stir often. Serve over pancakes. Makes about 2½ cups.

HAM AND MUSHROOM STUFFED PANCAKES

8 thin pancakes (about 7 inches in
diameter)
1 can (2 ounces) mushroom stems
and pieces, drained and chopped
2 tablespoons finely chopped onion
2 tablespoons butter or margarine
8 thin slices boiled ham
1 can (10¾ ounces) condensed
cream of celery soup
½ cup sour cream
¼ cup water
Paprika or chopped parsley

Prepare pancakes. In saucepan, cook mushrooms and onion in butter until onion is tender. Place a slice of ham and 2 teaspoons mushroom mixture on each pancake; roll. Keep warm in oven. Meanwhile, combine soup, sour cream, and water. Heat; stir occasionally. Serve sauce over pancakes. Garnish with paprika or chopped parsley. 4 servings.

CHINESE SHRIMP PANCAKES

8 thin pancakes
3 tablespoons thinly sliced green
onion
2 tablespoons butter or margarine
1 can (10¾ ounces) condensed
cream of chicken soup
1½ cups diced cooked shrimp
¼ cup sliced water chestnuts
¼ teaspoon soy sauce
¼ cup milk
¼ teaspoon Worcestershire
Dash hot pepper sauce

Prepare pancakes; keep warm. To make filling, in saucepan, cook green onion in butter until tender. Stir in ½ cup soup, shrimp, water chestnuts, and soy sauce. Heat; stir occasionally. To make sauce, combine remaining soup, milk, Worcestershire, and hot pepper sauce. Heat; stir occasionally. Place about ¼ cup filling on each pancake; roll up. Serve sauce over pancakes. 4 servings.

84

Surprise Cakes and Cookies

Tomato soup gives a wonder-what-it-is flavor and rosy color to cakes and cookies.

Once tried, these are the unusual cake specialties you will want to make again and again. Some women win blue ribbons at fairs with tomato soup cakes; others bake them for holiday gifts. Most women make them just for the pleasure of baking an easy cake with fascinating flavor—a little spicy, a little tangy, and altogether special.

Like the convenience of cake mixes? You can make a delicious, moist cake by adding a can of tomato soup and two eggs to a package of spice cake mix.

Or surprise everyone by giving a subtle new taste to those time-honored favorites, fruit cake and gingerbread. Tomato soup adds a distinctive flavor that'll have the family clamoring for more.

OLD FASHIONED GINGERBREAD CAKE

2 cans (10¾ ounces each) condensed tomato soup
3 eggs
2 packages (about 14 ounces each) gingerbread mix
1 cup raisins
1 cup chopped walnuts

In large bowl of mixer, blend soup and eggs. Add gingerbread mix. Blend at low speed until thoroughly moistened; beat 2 minutes on medium speed. Fold in raisins and walnuts. Pour into well-greased 10-inch tube pan. Bake at 325°F. for 1 hour 15 minutes or until cake is done. Cool right side up in pan 10 minutes; then remove from pan. Serve warm or cool. Sprinkle top with confectioners' sugar. Makes 10-inch tube cake.

GLAZE FOR OLD FASHIONED GINGERBREAD CAKE

1 **cup sifted confectioners' sugar**
2 **tablespoons rum**
1 **tablespoon melted butter**

Combine all ingredients; beat until smooth. Makes enough glaze for a 10-inch tube cake.

TOMATO SOUP CAKE

2¼ **cups cake flour or 2 cups**
    all-purpose flour
1⅓ **cups sugar**
4 **teaspoons baking powder**
1 **teaspoon baking soda**
1½ **teaspoons allspice**
1 **teaspoon cinnamon**
½ **teaspoon ground cloves**
1 **can (10¾ ounces) condensed**
    tomato soup
½ **cup hydrogenated shortening**
2 **eggs**
¼ **cup water**

Preheat oven to 350°F. Generously grease and flour two round layer pans, 8 or 9″ or an oblong pan, 13x9x2″. Measure dry ingredients into large bowl. Add soup and shortening. Beat at low to medium speed for 2 minutes (300 strokes with a spoon) scraping sides and bottom of bowl constantly. Add eggs and water. Beat 2 minutes more, scraping bowl frequently. Pour into pans. Bake 35 to 40 minutes. Let stand in pans 10 minutes; remove and cool on rack. Frost with Cream Cheese Frosting or favorite white frosting.

VARIATIONS: For a 9-inch tube pan. Prepare as above; bake 1 hour.
Nut or Raisin: After mixing, fold in 1 cup chopped nuts or 1 cup raisins. Bake 35 to 40 minutes.

Date and Nut: After mixing, fold in 1 cup chopped walnuts and 1 cup chopped dates. (Use 1 to 2 tablespoons flour to sprinkle over dates while chopping them.) Bake in 9″ layers or 13 x 9 x 2″ pan for 40 to 45 minutes.

CREAM CHEESE FROSTING

Blend 2 packages (3 ounces each) cream cheese (softened) with 1 tablespoon milk. Gradually add 1 package (1 pound) sifted confectioners' sugar; blend well. Mix in ½ teaspoon vanilla extract, if desired.

QUICK TOMATO SPICE CAKE

1 package (2 layer) spice cake mix
1 can (10¾ ounces) condensed
    tomato soup
½ cup water
2 eggs

Mix *only* above ingredients; following directions on package. If desired, fold in 1 cup chopped walnuts. Bake as directed. Frost with Cream Cheese Frosting. or other favorite white frosting.

EASY FRUIT CAKE

Prepare QUICK TOMATO SPICE CAKE. After mixing, fold in 1 cup chopped candied fruit and 1 cup chopped walnuts. Bake as directed on package adding about 5 minutes more.

FOR MINCEMEAT CAKE. Substitute ½ cup prepared mincemeat for candied fruit in EASY FRUIT CAKE. Bake in 9″ layers or 13 x 9 x 2″ pan.

APRICOT OR PRUNE UPSIDE-DOWN CAKE

Divide between two 9-inch round layer pans: ½ cup melted butter, ½ cup brown sugar; top with an arrangement of 1 can (1 pound) apricot halves, drained (about 1 cup) and ½ cup walnut pieces. Prepare QUICK TOMATO SPICE CAKE. Pour into pans spreading evenly over topping. Bake at 350°F. for 35 minutes. Run spatula around edge of pan. Immediately turn upside down on serving plate. Leave pan over cake 5 minutes. Serve warm or cooled.

FOR PRUNE CAKE: Follow directions above, substituting 1 jar or can (1 pound) canned pitted prunes, drained (about 1 cup) for apricots.

FOAMY SAUCE
(For Steamed Pudding)

1 egg, separated
¾ cup confectioners' sugar
¾ cup heavy cream, whipped
½ teaspoon vanilla extract

In small bowl of electric mixer, beat egg white until soft peaks form; *gradually* beat in sugar. Stir in egg yolk; fold in whipped cream and vanilla. Makes 2 cups.

STEAMED PUDDING

2½ cups sifted all-purpose flour
1 tablespoon baking powder
½ teaspoon baking soda
1 teaspoon ground cinnamon
½ teaspoon ground nutmeg
2 cups chopped dates
¼ cup shortening
1 cup sugar
1 egg
1 can (10¾ ounces) condensed
   tomato soup

Sift flour with baking powder, soda, and spices; dust dates with small amount of flour mixture. Cream shortening and sugar; add egg and mix well. Add dry ingredients alternately with soup; stir well after each addition. Fold in dates. Pour into greased 2-quart mold; cover securely with foil. Place on trivet in large pan. Add boiling water to one-half height of mold. Cover; steam 3 hours. Remove mold from water; uncover and loosen edges of pudding with knife. Unmold while hot. 12 servings. Serve with foamy sauce or hard sauce.

HARD SAUCE

⅓ cup soft butter
1 cup sifted confectioners' sugar
½ teaspoon vanilla extract

In bowl, soften butter. Add sugar, a little at a time; beat until creamy and smooth. Stir in vanilla extract. Chill until hard. ¾ cup sauce.

ROSY ROCK COOKIES

1½ cups all-purpose flour
1⅓ cups sugar
1 teaspoon baking powder
½ teaspoon baking soda
2 teaspoons cinnamon
1 teaspoon allspice
1 cup shortening
1 egg
1 can (10¾ ounces) condensed
   tomato soup
2 cups uncooked rolled oats
1 cup seedless raisins
1 cup chopped walnuts

Preheat oven to 350°F. Sift dry ingredients except oats together into large bowl. Add shortening, egg, and soup. Beat at medium speed for 2 minutes (300 strokes with a spoon), scraping sides and bottom of bowl constantly. Stir in oats, raisins, and nuts. Drop rounded teaspoonfuls on ungreased cookie sheet. Bake about 15 minutes or until lightly browned. Makes about 7 dozen cookies.

Party and International Specialties

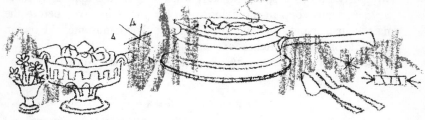

"Let's have a party."

Happy words indeed. And they lead to some of the most memorable occasions for everyone—when good friends get together.

What kind of party? Name almost any kind and good food will be a key factor to its success: Children's birthdays, holiday celebrations, anniversaries. Even when the girl next door comes for coffee, it can be a party.

TODAY'S SERVICE BUFFET STYLE

An easy style of service is a major requirement for today's parties because of smaller homes without dining rooms and little outside help. Buffet service is the answer for many a hostess. Nothing is more dazzling than a buffet table covered with colorful tempting foods. Each guest picks up a plate and helps himself while the hostess guides the proceedings.

Successful buffets are those where guests are at ease to enjoy the company and the food. Some pointers to follow are these:

1. Plan the menu with an eye for color. If the main dish is a casserole, top it with golden cheese or some slices of tomato or stuffed olives for that bit of color.
2. Serve at least one hot dish (perhaps a vegetable). Or if you're serving mainly hot foods, include relishes or a chilled fruit dessert for contrast.
3. Plan the food so the main course and accompaniments can all go on one's dinner plate. To achieve this, it's often helpful to serve vegetable relishes and spiced fruits instead of a salad.
4. Fork foods are best because guests won't have to worry about several pieces of silverware to juggle. Plan a meat that can be cut with a fork (for example—sliced ham or boned chicken); or use a main dish such as chicken à la king which requires no cutting.
5. Trays are helpful if guests do not sit at a table to eat.

BEAUTIFUL BEGINNINGS

Any party's off to a sparkling start when soup is the appetizer. Idea: serve a snappy soup in the living room for guests to savor before the main course. Now's the time to bring out that handsome old tureen and ladle or a lovely pitcher for pouring.

Select your soup from any of the recipes in the "Appetizer Soup" section. Or try one of these:

FRISKY SOUR

2 cans (10½ ounces each) condensed beef broth
1 soup can ice water
2 tablespoons lemon juice

Chill cans of soup in refrigerator 4 hours or more. Just before serving, combine all ingredients in a container; cover and shake. Serve in glasses. Makes about 4 cups.

FLAMING BEAN SOUP

2 cans (11 ounces each) condensed black bean soup
1 can (10½ ounces) condensed beef broth
2 soup cans water
¼ cup sherry or bourbon
Lemon slices

In saucepan, blend soups; add water. Heat; stir often. Pour into heat-proof chafing dish or tureen. To flame, heat the sherry or bourbon in a ladle. Put a lighted match to warmed liquor. While flaming, lower into the soup. Stir to blend the flavors before ladling out this warming brew. Pass lemon slices for garnish. Makes about 6½ cups.

TANGY SPLIT PEA BOWL

1 can (2 ounces) sliced mushrooms, drained
⅛ teaspoon thyme
1 tablespoon butter or margarine
1 can (11½ ounces) condensed split pea with ham soup
1 soup can water

In saucepan, lightly brown mushrooms with thyme in butter. Add soup; gradually stir in water. Heat; stir often. Makes about 2½ cups.

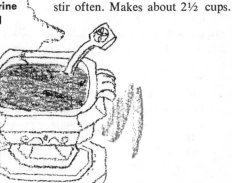

PARTY PATTERN SOUPS

Imagination often means the difference between an ordinary menu and one with party flair. Even a simple soup and sandwich meal can benefit from just a small touch of decoration. One easy-do soup garnish is croutons cut in various shapes to make Party Pattern Soups.

BRIDGE LUNCHEON: Cut white bread into bridge shapes (diamonds, hearts, clubs, and spades)—use small cookie cutters. Toast lightly and float one crouton on each bowl of cream soup.

Other party-pattern garnishes to try:
- Valentine's Day: Heart-shaped croutons.
- St. Patrick's Day: Shamrock-shaped croutons.
- July Fourth: Star-shaped croutons.
- Halloween: Pumpkin-shaped croutons.
- Christmas: Simple tree-shaped croutons.

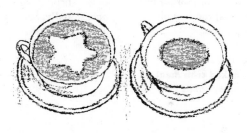

SPECIALTY DISHES

"Make one great dish your specialty"—good advice to hostesses everywhere. For many, it's the secret of their success. You can borrow from the great cooking of the world to make distinctive party fare—easily. Just look.

AFTER THE SHOW

Chilled V-8   Sesame Seed Wafers
Paella* or
Seafood Curry*
Mixed Green Salad
Pineapple Parfait   Fancy Cookies
Tea or Coffee

PAELLA

2 pounds chicken parts
2 tablespoons salad oil
1 can (10¾ ounces) condensed
  chicken broth
2 medium cloves garlic, minced
⅔ cup raw regular rice
½ cup chopped canned tomatoes
½ cup chopped green pepper
2 tablespoons chopped pimiento

In skillet, brown chicken in oil; pour off fat. Add broth and garlic. Cover; cook over low heat 15 minutes. Stir remaining ingredients into broth. Cover; cook 30 minutes more or until liquid is absorbed. Stir occasionally. 4 servings.

SEAFOOD CURRY

¼ cup chopped onion
1 teaspoon curry powder
1 tablespoon butter or margarine
1 can (10¾ ounces) condensed
  cream of celery soup
⅓ cup milk
1 cup diced cooked shrimp
½ cup flaked cooked crab meat
Cooked rice or patty shells

In saucepan, cook onion with curry in butter until tender. Add soup, milk, shrimp, and crab. Heat; stir occasionally. Serve over rice. Makes about 2½ cups.

JAMBALAYA

1 cup ham cut in strips
1 cup chopped onion
½ cup green pepper cut in squares
1 medium clove garlic, minced
2 tablespoons salad oil
1 can (10¾ ounces) condensed
  tomato soup
2 cups water
⅔ cup raw regular rice
1 medium bay leaf
Dash hot pepper sauce
1 cup cooked shrimp
Chopped parsley

In large skillet, brown ham and cook onion, green pepper, and garlic in oil until vegetables are tender. Add remaining ingredients except shrimp and parsley. Bring to a boil. Cover; cook over low heat 20 minutes. Stir occasionally. Stir in shrimp; cook 5 minutes more or until rice is tender. Garnish with parsley. Makes about 4½ cups.

A TOUCH OF PARIS

French Onion Soup* (see index)
Scallops Parisienne*
Buttered Green Peas
Endive Salad with Tomato French Dressing*
French Bread   Butter
Fruit Turnovers (from freezer)
Coffee

SCALLOPS PARISIENNE

1 pound fresh scallops
1 can (4 ounces) sliced mushrooms, drained
2 tablespoons chopped onion
2 tablespoons butter or margarine
1 can (11 ounces) condensed Cheddar cheese soup
2 teaspoons lemon juice
Dash pepper
Dash crushed thyme leaves
Dash ground marjoram
2 tablespoons buttered bread crumbs
Paprika

In saucepan, cook scallops in water over low heat for 10 minutes; drain well. Divide among 4 individual baking dishes. Meanwhile, in saucepan, brown mushrooms and cook onion in butter until tender. Add soup, lemon juice, and seasonings; pour over scallops. Top with crumbs; sprinkle with paprika. Bake at 350°F. for 30 minutes or until hot. 4 servings.

PILAF

½ cup fine egg noodles, broken in pieces
2 tablespoons butter or margarine
1 can (10¾ ounces) condensed chicken broth
⅓ cup water
½ cup raw regular rice

In saucepan, brown noodles in butter; stir often. Add remaining ingredients. Bring to a boil; stir. Cover; cook over low heat 20 to 25 minutes or until liquid is absorbed. Makes about 2 cups.

ARTICHOKE CASSEROLE

1 can (4 ounces) sliced mushrooms, drained
1 tablespoon butter or margarine
1 can (11 ounces) condensed Cheddar cheese soup
½ cup milk
2 tablespoons sherry
1½ cups cooked rice
1 package (10 ounces) artichoke hearts, cooked and drained
Paprika

In saucepan, brown mushrooms in butter; add soup, milk, and sherry. In 1-quart casserole, combine soup mixture, rice, and artichokes. Bake at 350°F. for 30 minutes; stir. Sprinkle with paprika. Makes about 4 cups.

SUPPER ITALIANO

Antipasto Tray
Chicken Cacciatore with Spaghetti*
Romaine Salad
Bread Sticks
Fruit   Cheese
Cafè Espresso

CHICKEN CACCIATORE

2 pounds chicken parts
2 tablespoons shortening
1 can (10¾ ounces) condensed tomato soup
¼ cup dry red wine or 1 tablespoon vinegar
½ cup chopped onion
2 large cloves garlic, minced
½ teaspoon oregano, crushed
⅛ teaspoon salt
½ medium green pepper, cut into strips

In skillet, brown chicken in shortening; pour off fat. Add remaining ingredients except pepper. Cover; cook over low heat 30 minutes; stir occasionally. Add pepper; cook 15 minutes more. 4 servings. Serve with spaghetti.

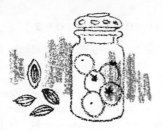

Supper Party Starter*
Curried Chicken*
Parsley Rice   Chutney
Jellied Vegetable Salad
Coconut Cake   Ice Cream
Coffee

CURRIED CHICKEN

2 pounds chicken parts
2 tablespoons shortening
1 can (10¾ ounces) condensed
   cream of chicken soup
½ cup chopped onion
1 to 2 tablespoons curry powder
Cooked rice
Chopped parsley

In skillet, brown chicken in shortening; pour off fat. Stir in soup, onion, and curry. Cover; cook over low heat 45 minutes or until chicken is tender. Stir occasionally. Serve with rice; garnish with parsley. Makes 4 servings.

CHICKEN PAPRIKA

2 pounds chicken parts
2 tablespoons shortening
1 can (10¾ ounces) condensed
   tomato soup
½ cup sour cream
1 can (4 ounces) sliced mushrooms,
   drained
¼ cup chopped onion
2 teaspoons paprika
1 medium bay leaf
Cooked noodles

In skillet, brown chicken in shortening; pour off fat. Add remaining ingredients except noodles. Cover; cook over low heat 45 minutes or until tender. Stir occasionally. Remove bay leaf. Serve with noodles. Makes 4 servings.

SOUPER SPAGHETTI 'N FRANKS

½ pound frankfurters, cut in
   1-inch pieces
½ cup chopped onion
1 teaspoon oregano leaves, crushed
2 tablespoons butter or margarine
1 can (11¼ ounces) condensed
   chili beef soup
1 can (15 ounces) spaghetti in
   tomato sauce with cheese

In saucepan, brown frankfurters and cook onion with oregano in butter until tender. Stir in soup and spaghetti. Heat; stir occasionally. Makes about 3½ cups.

BREAST OF CHICKEN MAGNIFIQUE

4 whole chicken breasts
(about 3 pounds), split
2 tablespoons shortening
2 cans (10¾ ounces each)
condensed cream of chicken soup
2 cups sliced fresh mushrooms
(about ½ pound)
1 large clove garlic, minced
Generous dash crushed thyme leaves
⅛ teaspoon crushed rosemary
leaves
Cooked long grain and wild rice mix

Use 1 large skillet or prepare in 2 skillets (10-inch) by dividing ingredients equally. Brown chicken in shortening; pour off fat. Stir in soup, mushrooms, garlic, and seasonings. Cover; cook over low heat 30 minutes or until chicken is tender. Stir occasionally. Serve with rice. Makes 8 servings.

CHICKEN VIA VENETO

4 pounds chicken parts
¼ cup butter or margarine
1 cup ham strips
2 cans (11 ounces each) condensed Cheddar cheese soup
½ cup chopped canned tomatoes
3 medium onions, quartered
½ teaspoon basil, crushed

Use 1 large skillet or prepare in 2 skillets (about 10-inch) by dividing ingredients equally. Brown chicken in butter; remove. Brown ham. Stir in soup, tomatoes, onions, and basil; add chicken. Cover; cook over low heat 45 minutes or until tender. Stir occasionally. 8 servings.

CHINESE HOT POT

2 chicken breasts (about 1½ pounds), split, skinned, and boned
1 pound asparagus, cut diagonally in 1-inch pieces
½ pound thinly sliced mushrooms (about 2 cups)
1 package (1 pound) spinach, cleaned
2 cans (10¾ ounces each) condensed chicken broth
2 soup cans water
Soy sauce
1 cup cooked rice

Cut chicken into thin strips. On serving platter, arrange chicken, asparagus, mushrooms, and spinach. Prepare at table in 10-inch skillet over direct heat or an electric skillet. Combine broth and water; heat to boiling. Add half of the chicken, asparagus, and mushrooms; cook over low heat 3 minutes. Add half of the spinach; cook 2 minutes more or until just done. Remove with slotted spoon and serve with soy. Meanwhile, cook remaining chicken and vegetables as above. Add rice to remaining broth. Heat; serve in soup bowls. 4 servings.

NEAR EAST MEATBALLS

1 pound ground beef
¼ cup fine dry bread crumbs
1 egg, slightly beaten
3 teaspoons Worcestershire
½ teaspoon salt
1 can (10½ ounces) condensed
   onion soup
1 soup can water
1 cup raw regular rice
1 can (about 4 ounces) sliced
   mushrooms, drained
Chopped parsley

Mix thoroughly beef, crumbs, egg, 2 teaspoons Worcestershire, and salt. Shape into 16 meatballs. In skillet, brown meatballs (use shortening if necessary); pour off fat. Add soup, water, rice, mushrooms, and remaining Worcestershire. Bring to boil; cover. Reduce heat; simmer 20 minutes or until rice is done. Stir often. Garnish with parsley. Makes about 5½ cups.

QUICK LASAGNE

½ pound ground beef
1 cup chopped onion
2 large cloves garlic, minced
2 teaspoons oregano, crushed
2 cans (10¾ ounces each)
   condensed tomato soup
½ cup water
2 teaspoons vinegar
½ pound plain lasagne
   noodles, cooked and drained
1 pint cottage cheese or ricotta
½ pound Mozzarella cheese,
   thinly sliced
Grated Parmesan cheese

In saucepan, brown beef and cook onion, garlic, oregano. Add soup, water, vinegar. Simmer 30 minutes; stir occasionally. In baking dish (12x8x2"), arrange 3 alternate layers of noodles, cottage cheese, meat sauce, Mozzarella. Top with Parmesan. Bake at 350°F. for 30 minutes. Let stand 15 minutes. 6 servings.

MOCK SUKIYAKI

1 pound boneless round steak
   (¾" thick)
1½ cups sliced celery
1 medium green pepper,
   cut in 1-inch pieces
1½ cups sliced fresh mushrooms
   (about ¼ pound)
1 large onion, thinly sliced
2 tablespoons salad oil
1 can (10½ ounces) condensed
   beef broth
1 tablespoon soy sauce
2 tablespoons cornstarch
Cooked rice

Freeze meat 1 hour to firm (makes slicing easier); slice into very thin strips. In skillet, cook celery, pepper, mushrooms, and onion in oil until *just* tender; push to one side. Add meat; cook until color changes (about 3 to 4 minutes). Add broth, soy, and cornstarch. Cook, stirring until thickened. Serve with rice and additional soy sauce. Makes about 4½ cups.

Pork Chops with Party Hats*
Scalloped Potatoes* (see index)   Brussels Sprouts
Apple and Nut Salad   Muffins
Birthday Cake
Coffee   Milk

PORK CHOPS WITH PARTY HATS

6 pork chops (about 1½ pounds)
Salt and pepper
6 onion slices
6 green pepper rings
1 can (10¾ ounces) condensed tomato soup

In oven-proof skillet, brown chops; pour off fat. Season with salt and pepper. Place slice of onion and pepper ring on each; pour soup over. Cover; bake at 350°F. for 45 minutes or until chops are tender. 4 servings.

VEAL SWISS STYLE

1½ pounds thinly sliced veal cutlet
3 slices (4 ounces) Swiss cheese, cut in half
3 slices (4 ounces) boiled ham, cut in half
4 tablespoons butter or margarine
1 can (10¾ ounces) condensed cream of mushroom soup
¼ teaspoon paprika
½ cup milk
¼ cup sauterne or other dry white wine

Cut veal into 12 oblong pieces; pound with meat hammer. On each of 6 pieces place ½ slice cheese and ham; top with remaining veal. Fasten securely with toothpicks. In large skillet, brown veal in butter. Stir in remaining ingredients. Cook over low heat 30 minutes or until tender; stir occasionally. 6 servings.

HOME-STYLE POT ROAST

3-pound boneless pot roast
2 tablespoons shortening
1 can (10½ ounces) condensed beef broth
2 medium onions, quartered
½ teaspoon salt
⅛ teaspoon pepper
1 large bay leaf
6 medium potatoes, cut in half (about 2 pounds)
6 medium carrots, cut in 2-inch pieces
½ cup water
¼ cup flour

In large heavy pan, brown meat on all sides in shortening; pour off fat. Add broth, onion, and seasonings. Cover; cook over low heat 2 hours. Add potatoes and carrots. Cook 1 hour more or until tender; stir occasionally. Remove bay leaf. Gradually blend water into flour until smooth; slowly stir into sauce. Cook, stirring until thickened. Makes 6 to 8 servings.

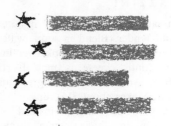

U.S.A.—ALL THE WAY

Cream of Mushroom Soup
Saucy Sirloin*
Hot Rice   Green Beans Amandine
Assorted Relishes
Brown 'n Serve Rolls   Butter
Apple Strudel (from freezer)
Coffee

SAUCY SIRLOIN

1½ pounds sirloin steak
(¾" thick)
2 tablespoons salad oil
1 can (10½ ounces) condensed
consommé
¼ cup Burgundy or other dry
red wine
½ cup diagonally sliced green
onion (1" pieces)
1 can (4 ounces) sliced mushrooms,
drained
1 teaspoon Worcestershire
Dash dry mustard

Freeze meat 1 hour to firm (makes slicing easier); slice into very thin strips. In skillet, cook meat in oil until color changes (about 3 to 4 minutes); pour off fat. Add remaining ingredients. Cook, stirring until thickened. Serve over rice. Makes about 4 cups.

ARROZ CON POLLO

2 pounds chicken parts
2 tablespoons salad oil
1 can (10¾ ounces) condensed
chicken broth
1 can (1 pound) tomatoes, cut up
⅓ cup water
½ cup chopped onion
2 medium cloves garlic, minced
1 teaspoon salt
¼ teaspoon saffron or turmeric
⅛ teaspoon pepper
1 bay leaf
1 package (10 ounces) frozen peas
1 cup raw regular rice
¼ cup sliced stuffed or ripe olives

In skillet, brown chicken in oil; pour off fat. Add broth, tomatoes, water, onion, garlic, salt, saffron, pepper, and bay. Cover; cook over low heat 15 minutes. Add remaining ingredients. Cover; cook 30 minutes more or until chicken and rice are tender; stir occasionally. Remove bay leaf. 4 servings.

99

PARTY TETRAZZINI

2 tablespoons chopped onion
1 tablespoon butter or margarine
1 can (10¾ ounces) condensed
  cream of mushroom soup
½ cup water
½ cup shredded sharp process
  cheese
1 tablespoon sherry (optional)
2 cups cooked spaghetti
1½ cups cubed cooked chicken
  or turkey
2 tablespoons chopped pimiento
1 tablespoon chopped parsley

In saucepan, cook onion in butter until tender. Blend in soup, water, cheese, and sherry. Cook over low heat until cheese is melted; stir often. Add remaining ingredients; heat. Makes about 3½ cups.
NOTE: For variety, instead of chicken in above recipe, brown 1 cup finely diced cooked ham along with onion; then prepare as directed.

GLAZED COLD MEATS

Have you ever wanted to set out a platter of cold meats for a crowd and then been disappointed to see how quickly they dry and curl? Try this simple attractive and delicious way to glaze a mixed platter of cold cuts, so that they may be arranged in advance.

1 envelope unflavored gelatine
½ cup cold water
1 can (10½ ounces) condensed
  consommé
1 teaspoon Worcestershire
2 teaspoons lemon juice
16 slices cooked ham, beef, tongue,
  or turkey (about 1½ pounds)
Cucumber slices
Cherry tomatoes, cut in half
1 hard-cooked egg, sliced

In saucepan, sprinkle gelatine on cold water to soften. Place over low heat, stirring until gelatine is dissolved. Remove from heat; stir in consommé, Worcestershire, and lemon juice. Chill until slightly thickened. Meanwhile, on 12-inch round platter, arrange overlapping slices of meat and cucumbers. Place tomatoes around edge and egg in center. Spoon a thin layer of gelatine mixture over entire platter. Chill until set. Makes 8 servings.

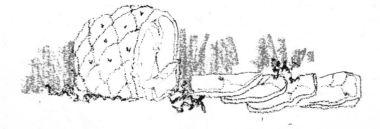

SENSATIONAL SALADS

Need a show-stopper? Serve a shimmering gelatine salad, molded to perfection and nestled regally on a bed of crisp greens. Surely the pièce de résistance for any summer luncheon!

Here's a simple pattern menu—with endless variations—featuring a superb molded main dish salad.

FAVORITE SALAD LUNCHEON

Rumaki
Hawaiian Chicken Velvet Salad*
Asparagus Spears   Hot Rolls
Sherbet   Angel Food Cake
Coffee or Tea

HAWAIIAN CHICKEN VELVET SALAD

1 can (about 8 ounces) crushed pineapple in syrup
1 envelope unflavored gelatine
1 can (10¾ ounces) condensed cream of chicken soup
1 package (3 ounces) cream cheese, softened
1 tablespoon lemon juice
Dash ground ginger
1 cup diced cooked chicken
¼ cup chopped celery
Toasted slivered almonds

Drain pineapple, saving ⅓ cup syrup. In saucepan, sprinkle gelatine on pineapple syrup to soften. Place over low heat, stirring until gelatine is dissolved. Remove from heat. Gradually blend soup into cream cheese until smooth; slowly stir in gelatine mixture, lemon juice, and ginger. Chill until slightly thickened; fold in chicken, celery, and pineapple. Pour into a 1-quart mold; chill 4 hours or until firm. Unmold on crisp salad greens; garnish with almonds. Makes about 3 cups.

BEEF TOMATO SALAD

2 envelopes unflavored gelatine
1½ cups water
1 bay leaf
1 can (10½ ounces) condensed consommé
1 can (10¾ ounces) condensed tomato soup
2 tablespoons vinegar
⅛ teaspoon celery salt
1 cup finely chopped cooked beef
½ cup chopped celery
¼ cup chopped cucumber
2 tablespoons chopped onion

In saucepan, sprinkle gelatine on water to soften. Add bay leaf. Place over low heat and stir until gelatine is dissolved. Remove from heat and stir in soups, vinegar, and celery salt. Remove bay leaf. Chill until mixture begins to thicken. Fold in remaining ingredients. Pour into 5½-cup mold. Chill until firm. Unmold; serve on crisp salad greens. Makes about 5 cups.

Special Occasion Meats

BEEF ITALIANO

1 boneless chuck (about 3½ pounds)
1 cup sliced onion
1 large clove garlic, minced
2 teaspoons oregano, crushed
1 can (10¾ ounces) condensed tomato soup
½ cup water
Generous dash pepper

Trim fat from meat; place in roasting pan. Bake at 350°F. for 1 hour. Spoon off fat. Combine remaining ingredients; pour over meat. Cover; bake 2 hours more or until tender. Thicken sauce if desired. 6 servings.

STEWED CHICKEN WITH DUMPLINGS

2 pounds chicken parts
2 tablespoons shortening
1 can (10¾ ounces) condensed cream of chicken soup
½ cup water
4 small carrots, cut in 2-inch pieces
1 medium onion, thickly sliced
½ cup celery cut in 2-inch pieces
Dash pepper
1 cup biscuit mix
⅓ cup milk

In large heavy pan, brown chicken in shortening; pour off fat. Add soup, water, vegetables, and pepper. Cover; cook over low heat 30 minutes. Stir occasionally. Meanwhile, combine biscuit mix and milk with fork. Drop by spoonfuls onto pieces of chicken. Cook uncovered 10 minutes. Cover; cook 10 minutes more or until dumplings are done. Makes 4 servings.

SOUPER TUNA LOAF

1 can (10¾ ounces) condensed tomato soup
2 cans (about 7 ounces each) tuna, drained and flaked
1 cup small bread cubes
2 eggs, slightly beaten
2 tablespoons chopped parsley
2 teaspoons lemon juice
2 tablespoons water
1 tablespoon prepared horseradish
⅛ teaspoon basil leaves, crushed

Mix thoroughly ½ cup soup, tuna, bread cubes, egg, parsley, and lemon juice. Spread evenly in well-greased loaf pan (8x4x3"). Bake at 400°F. for 40 minutes. Loosen edges; unmold. Meanwhile, combine remaining ingredients. Heat; stir occasionally. Serve with loaf. Makes 6 servings.

CHICKEN MARSALA

3 whole chicken breasts (about
   2½ pounds), split
2 tablespoons butter or margarine
1 can (10¾ ounces) condensed
   cream of mushroom soup
⅓ cup water
2 tablespoons Marsala
1 teaspoon lemon juice
1 large clove garlic, minced
½ teaspoon paprika
Dash pepper

In skillet, slowly cook chicken in butter until done (about 30 minutes). Remove chicken to heated platter. Stir remaining ingredients into drippings. Heat; stir occasionally. Serve over chicken. Makes 6 servings.

PORK GOULASH

1½ pounds lean pork cubes
   (1½-inch)
2 tablespoons shortening
1 can (10½ ounces) condensed
   onion soup
1 can (16 ounces) tomatoes, cut up
¼ cup chopped celery
½ teaspoon garlic salt
⅛ teaspoon ground thyme
Dash pepper
1 small green pepper, cut in strips
¼ cup water
2 tablespoons flour
Cooked noodles

In skillet, brown meat in shortening; pour off fat. Add soup, tomatoes, celery, and seasonings. Cover; cook over low heat 2 hours 15 minutes. Add green pepper; cook 15 minutes more or until meat is tender. Stir occasionally. Gradually blend water into flour until smooth; slowly stir into sauce. Cook, stirring until thickened. Serve over noodles. Makes about 5 cups.

MARDI GRAS CHICKEN LIVERS

1 package (8 ounces) frozen
   chicken livers, thawed
½ cup thinly sliced onion
⅓ cup thinly sliced celery
2 tablespoons butter or margarine
1 can (10¾ ounces) condensed
   tomato soup
¼ cup chopped parsley
¼ cup water
¼ teaspoon lemon juice
Cooked rice

In saucepan, cook livers, onion, and celery in butter until done. Add soup, parsley, water, and lemon juice. Heat; stir occasionally. Serve over rice. Makes about 2½ cups.

Cooking for a Crowd

What do a gala party and a church supper have in common? Good food and plenty of people.

When it's your turn to cook, relax. It's easy to serve large-scale dishes with ease if you plan ahead foods that are readily made in quantity. Soup is an ideal first course. It can help out behind the scenes, too, in making enticing main dishes and tasty vegetables that cater happily to a crowd.

FLEET'S-IN CHOWDER

4 cans (10¾ ounces each) condensed Manhattan clam chowder
3 soup cans water
2 pounds fillet of white fish, cut in 2-inch pieces
2 tablespoons chopped parsley
2 medium bay leaves
1 teaspoon thyme leaves, crushed
⅛ teaspoon garlic powder

In large saucepan, combine all ingredients. Bring to boil; reduce heat. Simmer 10 minutes or until fish is done. Stir occassionally. Remove bay leaves. Makes about 10 cups.

HARVEST SOUP

3 cans (10¾ ounces each) condensed cream of chicken soup
3 cans (10¾ ounces each) condensed tomato soup
8 soup cans water
3 cans (10¾ ounces each) condensed chicken gumbo soup

In large saucepan, combine cream of chicken soup and tomato soup; stir until smooth. Blend in water and chicken gumbo soup. Heat; stir occasionally. Makes about 20 cups.

FROSTY FLING

3 cans (10¾ ounces each)
  condensed tomato soup
2 cans (10½ ounces each)
  condensed beef broth
3 soup cans water
1 teaspoon Worcestershire
⅛ teaspoon hot pepper sauce

In large saucepan, combine all ingredients. Heat; stir occasionally. Chill overnight. Serve in chilled bowls. Makes about 10 cups.

FAR EASTERN CHICKEN POT

4 cans (10¾ ounces each)
  condensed cream of chicken soup
4 soup cans milk
2 tablespoons chopped parsley
Generous dash ground cloves
⅛ teaspoon ground nutmeg
⅛ teaspoon hot pepper sauce
¼ cup toasted slivered almonds

In large saucepan, blend soup; gradually stir in milk. Add remaining ingredients except almonds. Heat; stir occasionally. Garnish with almonds. Makes about 10 cups.

FAVORITE BEAN SOUP

7 cans (11½ ounces each)
  condensed bean with bacon soup
5 soup cans water
2 cans (16 ounces each) tomatoes,
  chopped
2 packages (10 ounces each)
  frozen lima beans, cooked
  and drained
2 tablespoons Worcestershire

In large saucepan, blend soup; gradually stir in water. Add remaining ingredients. Heat; stir occasionally. Makes about 22½ cups.

CHICKEN A LA KING

½ cup diced green pepper
¼ cup butter or margarine
6 cans (10¾ ounces each)
  condensed cream of chicken soup
2 to 3 cups milk
1½ quarts diced cooked chicken
¼ cup chopped pimiento
⅛ teaspoon pepper
Toast or patty shells

In large saucepan, cook green pepper in butter until tender. Gradually blend in soup and milk; stir until smooth. Add chicken, pimiento, and pepper. Heat slowly; stir occasionally. Serve on toast or in patty shells. Makes about 13 cups.

PARTY-SIZE GREEN BEAN CASSEROLE

3 cans (10¾ ounces each)
   condensed cream of mushroom
   soup
1½ cups milk
1 tablespoon soy sauce
¼ teaspoon pepper
9 cups cooked drained French style
   green beans
3 cans (3½ ounces each)
   French fried onions

In large bowl, stir soup; gradually blend in milk, soy sauce, and pepper. Add beans and 1½ cans onions. Spoon into three 1½-quart casseroles. Bake at 350°F. for 25 minutes or until hot; stir. Top with remaining onions; bake 5 minutes more. Makes about 12 cups.

BAKED TUNA 'N NOODLES

2 cups thinly sliced celery
½ cup chopped onion
4 tablespoons butter or margarine
6 cans (10¾ ounces each)
   condensed cream of mushroom
   soup
3 cups milk
6 cups cooked noodles
6 cans (about 7 ounces each) tuna,
   drained and flaked
½ cup diced pimiento
½ cup buttered bread crumbs

In large saucepan, cook celery and onion in butter until tender. Blend in soup; gradually stir in milk. Add noodles, tuna, and pimiento. Pour into four 1½-quart casseroles or five 1½-quart shallow baking dishes (10x6x2" each). Bake at 400°F. for 20 minutes or until hot; stir. Top with crumbs; bake 5 minutes more. Makes about 20 cups.

STUFFED TURKEY

6 slices bacon
1 cup sliced celery
½ cup chopped onion
1 package (8 ounces) herb seasoned stuffing mix
2 cups coarse corn bread crumbs
1 can (10¾ ounces) condensed chicken broth
1 egg, slightly beaten
10-pound turkey
1 can (10¾ ounces) condensed cream of mushroom soup
½ cup whole berry cranberry sauce
¼ cup orange juice

In skillet, cook bacon until crisp; remove and crumble. Pour off all but 2 tablespoons drippings. Cook celery and onion in drippings until tender. Toss lightly with stuffing mix, corn bread, broth, and egg. Fill cavity of turkey loosely with stuffing. Truss; place in roasting pan. Cover with foil. Roast at 325°F. for about 4 hours (25 minutes per pound or until tender). Uncover last hour to brown. Remove turkey to serving platter. Skim fat from drippings; add remaining ingredients. Heat; stir to loosen browned bits. 8 to 10 servings.

CHICKEN SUPREME

5 pounds chicken parts
¼ cup melted butter or margarine
3 cans (10¾ ounces each) condensed cream of chicken or mushroom soup
1 teaspoon paprika
⅛ teaspoon pepper

In shallow roasting pan (18x12x2") or two (13x9x2" each), arrange chicken in single layer skin-side down. Pour butter over chicken. Bake at 400°F. for 25 minutes. Turn chicken; bake 25 minutes more. Blend soup, paprika, and pepper; pour over chicken. Bake 20 minutes more or until chicken is tender. Makes 8 servings.

BEEF ROULADES

4 pounds thinly sliced round steak
4 cups prepared packaged herb seasoned stuffing mix
¼ cup shortening
2 cans (10¾ ounces each) condensed cream of mushroom soup
1 cup water

Cut steak into 16 long pieces; pound with meat hammer. Place ¼ cup stuffing on each piece of steak; roll up; fasten with toothpicks. In large skillet, brown in shortening; pour off fat. Stir in soup, water. Cover; simmer 1½ hours or until tender. Stir occasionally. Uncover; cook until desired consistency. 16 servings.

For Teens Only

If you like your food fun, fast, and lip-smackin' good—read on. These recipes have a knack for making everything from snacks to supper dishes into something special.

Discover fantastic soups—hot and cold; hearty sandwiches—quick and easy; greats from the grill—yummy. All depend on one versatile ingredient—condensed soup—for lively taste and care-free cooking. Happy eating, everyone!

AFTER-SKATING WARM-UP

Mugs of Chickety Chick*
Cheese and Crackers
Apples   Oatmeal Cookies

CHICKETY CHICK

1 can (10¾ ounces) condensed
  cream of chicken soup
1 soup can water
¼ teaspoon poultry seasoning

In saucepan, combine all ingredients. Heat; stir often. Sip from heavy cups or mugs. Makes about 2½ cups.

VACATION SPECIAL

Watch your P's and Q's while school's out

1 can (10¾ ounces) condensed
  tomato soup
1 soup can water
¼ cup cooked alphabet noodles

In saucepan, blend soup and water; add noodles. Heat. Makes about 2½ cups.

CHILI BEEF FRANKS

¼ pound ground beef
1 can (11¼ ounces) condensed
    chili beef soup
⅓ cup water
2 teaspoons prepared mustard
1 pound frankfurters, cooked
10 frankfurter buns, slit and toasted

In saucepan, brown beef; stir to separate meat. Add soup, water, and mustard. Heat; stir often. Place frankfurters in buns. Spoon soup mixture over. Makes 10 sandwiches.

CREAMY PEANUT BUTTER SOUP

1 can (10¾ ounces) condensed
    tomato soup
¼ cup peanut butter (chunky or
    smooth)
1½ soup cans milk

In saucepan, stir soup into peanut butter, a little at a time, until well blended; add milk. Heat; stir occasionally. Makes about 3 cups.

SUMMERTIME SPECIAL
Great after a swim

1 can (11¼ ounces) condensed
    green pea soup
1 can (10¾ ounces) condensed
    cream of potato soup
2 soup cans water or milk
⅛ teaspoon thyme leaves, crushed
Dash ground nutmeg

In saucepan, combine all ingredients. Heat; stir occasionally. Makes about 5 cups.

WINTERTIME TREAT
Warms nose and toes

1 can (about 2¼ ounces)
    deviled ham
1 teaspoon chopped parsley
3 melba toast rounds
¼ cup chopped onion
1 tablespoon butter or margarine
1 can (11¼ ounces) condensed
    green pea soup
½ soup can milk
½ soup can water

Combine 1 tablespoon ham and parsley. Spread on melba toast. Arrange on cookie sheet. Broil 4 inches from heat 2 minutes or until hot. Meanwhile, in saucepan, cook onion in butter until tender. Blend in soup and remaining ham; gradually stir in milk and water. Heat; stir occasionally. Garnish with melba toast. Makes about 2½ cups.

SLOPPY JOSÉS

South of the border sloppy Joes!

1 pound ground beef
1 cup chopped onion
1 cup chopped celery
1 teaspoon chili powder
½ teaspoon salt
Dash pepper
1 tablespoon shortening
1 can (10¾ ounces) condensed
tomato soup
6 buns, split and toasted

Brown beef with onion, celery, and seasonings in shortening; stir to separate meat. Add soup; simmer to blend flavors. Serve on buns. Makes about 3 cups.

HOME-FROM-THE-GAME SUPPER

Frankburgers*
Celery and Carrot Sticks   Pickles
Milk
Fresh Fruit   Pretzels

FRANKBURGERS

1 can (10¾ ounces) condensed
tomato soup
1½ pounds ground beef
1 teaspoon salt
⅛ teaspoon pepper
1½ teaspoons chili powder
6 frankfurter buns, split and toasted
6 frankfurters, split lengthwise
½ cup chopped onion
2 tablespoons chopped green
pepper
2 tablespoons butter or margarine
1 tablespoon brown sugar
1 teaspoon vinegar

Combine ⅓ cup soup, beef, salt, pepper, and 1 teaspoon chili powder; mix thoroughly. Spread meat mixture evenly over buns; *cover edges completely.* Firmly press 2 frankfurter halves, cut side up, into the center of each bun half. Bake on broiler pan at 450°F. for 12-15 minutes. Meanwhile, in saucepan, cook onion and green pepper with remaining chili powder in butter until tender. Stir in remaining soup, sugar, and vinegar. Heat; stir occasionally. Serve over sandwiches. Makes 6 open-face sandwiches.

110

Pizza Doggies*
Raw Vegetable Tray
Doughnuts
Cream Soda Shake

PIZZA DOGGIES

1 large clove garlic, minced
2 tablespoons olive oil
1 can (10¾ ounces) condensed
   tomato soup
¼ cup water
2 tablespoons chopped parsley
¼ teaspoon oregano leaves,
   crushed
1 pound frankfurters, slit
1 cup shredded Mozzarella cheese
10 frankfurter buns, slit and toasted

In saucepan, cook garlic in oil. Add soup, water, parsley, and oregano; cook over low heat 15 minutes. Stir occasionally. Meanwhile, broil frankfurters 4 inches from heat for 10 minutes or until done. Top with cheese; broil until cheese melts. Serve in buns with sauce. Makes 10 sandwiches.

PRONTO CHILI

1 can (11¼ ounces) condensed
   chili beef soup
½ soup can water

Empty soup into saucepan; gradually blend in water. Heat; stir often. Makes about 1½ cups.

BACON-TOMATO BROIL

4 slices toast
4 slices tomato
8 slices bacon, cooked and
   cut in half
1 can (10¾ ounces) condensed
   cream of mushroom soup
⅓ cup milk
1 teaspoon finely chopped onion
½ teaspoon Worcestershire

In shallow baking dish (13x9x2"), arrange toast; top with tomato and bacon. In bowl, blend soup and remaining ingredients; spread over sandwiches; *cover edges completely.* Broil 4 inches from heat 5 minutes or until hot. Makes 4 open-face sandwiches.

111

Chilled Cranberry Juice
Special Chicken Stack*
Fresh Fruit Cup
Rosy Rocks*
Milk and Coffee

SPECIAL CHICKEN STACK

¼ cup chopped onion
2 tablespoons butter or margarine
1 can (10¾ ounces) condensed
  cream of chicken soup
⅓ cup milk
1 can (5 ounces) boned chicken
  or turkey, cut up
2 hard-cooked eggs, sliced
1 package (9 ounces) frozen
  French style green beans,
  cooked and drained
4 slices toast

In saucepan, cook onion in butter until tender; blend in soup, milk, chicken, and eggs (save several slices of egg for garnish). Heat; stir occasionally. Place a mound of hot green beans on each slice toast; spoon creamed chicken over all. Garnish with egg slices. Makes 4 open-face sandwiches.

BEAN 'N CORNED BEEF SPREAD

1 can (11½ ounces) condensed
  bean with bacon soup
1 cup chopped cooked corned beef
⅓ cup water
1 teaspoon prepared horseradish
1 teaspoon prepared mustard

In saucepan, combine all ingredients. Spread on crunchy buttered rolls. Makes about 2 cups.

PERRITOS CON CHILE

For starving he-men

½ pound frankfurters, cut in
  ½-inch slices
½ cup chopped onion
2 tablespoons chopped
  green pepper
½ teaspoon chili powder
2 tablespoons butter or margarine
2 cans (1 pound 4 ounces each)
  kidney beans, drained
1 can (10¾ ounces) condensed
  tomato soup
1 teaspoon vinegar
½ teaspoon Worcestershire

In saucepan, cook frankfurters, onion, green pepper, and chili powder in butter until franks are browned. Add remaining ingredients. Cover; cook over low heat 12 to 15 minutes. Stir often. Makes about 3½ cups. Serve with crunchy Italian bread, cheese, and a crisp salad.

SEE YOU IN SEPTEMBER

Bean 'n Bacon Burgers*
All the Trimmings
Deviled Eggs
Potato Chips
Lemonade
Homemade Ice Cream

BEAN 'N BACON BURGERS

1 pound ground beef
¼ cup chopped onion
2 tablespoons chopped green
pepper
1 can (11½ ounces) condensed
bean with bacon soup
½ cup water
⅓ cup ketchup
6 hamburger buns, split and
toasted

In saucepan, brown beef and cook onion and green pepper until tender (use shortening if necessary); stir to separate meat. Add soup, water, and ketchup; simmer about 5 minutes to blend flavors. Stir often. (Thin to desired consistency with additional water.) Serve on buns. Makes about 3 cups.

MEXICALI SUPPER

2 slices bacon
¼ cup green pepper, cut into
1-inch strips
1 can (11¼ ounces) condensed
chili beef soup
½ soup can water
⅓ cup shredded mild process cheese

In saucepan, cook bacon until crisp. Remove; drain and crumble. Pour off all but 1 tablespoon drippings; add green pepper and cook until tender. Stir in soup; gradually blend in water. Add cheese. Heat until cheese melts; stir often. Top with bacon. Makes about 2 cups.

SUNBATHER'S SIPPER

Enjoy while you soak up the sun—or warm up after a cold dip

1 can (10½ ounces) condensed
beef broth
½ soup can apple juice
Dash ground cinnamon or nutmeg,
if desired

Mix ingredients and pour over ice cubes, or heat and serve hot. Makes about 1½ cups.

Sandwiches—Hot and Heroic

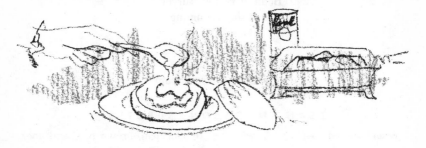

The sandwich has come a long way since the Earl of Sandwich asked for a slice of meat between two slices of bread. Now your favorite sandwich may make a hot and hearty lunch dish or a satisfying evening snack.

Bring it toasted and bubbling from the grill or spoon on an enticing filling. Either way, with condensed soup as an ingredient, it's a feast-on-bread.

BROILED EGG SALAD SANDWICH

1 can (10¾ ounces) condensed cream of mushroom soup
4 hard-cooked eggs, chopped
½ cup finely chopped celery
2 tablespoons finely chopped onion
1 tablespoon sweet pickle relish
1 teaspoon prepared mustard
Dash pepper
4 frankfurter buns, split and toasted

Combine soup, eggs, celery, onion, relish, mustard, and pepper. Spread mixture evenly over bun halves; *cover edges completely.* Broil about 4 inches from heat until hot, about 7 minutes. 4 open-face sandwiches.

TOMATO CHEESE 'N BACON BROIL

8 slices (about 8 ounces) process cheese
8 slices toast
1 can (10¾ ounces) condensed tomato soup
8 slices bacon, partially cooked and cut in half

Place a slice of cheese on each slice of toast; spread with soup; *cover edges completely.* Top with bacon. Broil 4 inches from heat until bacon is done. Makes 8 open-face sandwiches.

TUNABURGERS

4 slices toast
1 can (about 7 ounces) tuna, drained and flaked
4 onion slices
2 hard-cooked eggs, sliced
1 can (10¾ ounces) condensed cream of celery soup
⅓ cup milk
2 tablespoons chopped parsley
2 teaspoons lemon juice

Arrange toast on cookie sheet or in shallow baking pan; top with tuna, onion, and egg. Combine remaining ingredients; pour over sandwiches. Broil 4 inches from heat 5 minutes or until hot. Makes 4 open-face sandwiches.

WESTERN BURGER

½ cup chopped cooked ham
¼ cup coarsely chopped green pepper
¼ cup chopped onion
2 tablespoons butter or margarine
1 can (10¾ ounces) condensed cream of mushroom soup
6 eggs, slightly beaten
Dash pepper
6 hamburger buns, split and toasted

In skillet, brown ham and cook green pepper and onion in butter until tender. Blend soup, eggs, and pepper; add to ham mixture. Cook over low heat. As mixture begins to set around edges, gently lift cooked portions with large turner so that thin, uncooked portions can flow to the bottom. Continue gently lifting cooked portions until eggs are completely set, but still moist. Serve on buns. Makes 6 servings.

CHILIBURGER

1 pound ground beef
1 tablespoon shortening
1 can (11½ ounces) condensed bean with bacon soup
½ cup ketchup
½ teaspoon chili powder
6 buns, split and toasted

In skillet, brown beef in shortening; stir to separate meat. Add soup, ketchup, and chili powder; simmer about 5 minutes to blend flavors. Stir often. (Add a little water, if desired.) Serve on buns. Makes about 3 cups.

HORSERADISH SOUPERBURGER

1 pound ground beef
1 can (10¾ ounces) condensed cream of mushroom soup
½ cup sour cream
1 teaspoon prepared horseradish
¼ cup chopped green pepper or pimiento
6 buns, split and toasted

Brown beef in skillet; stir to separate meat. Add soup, sour cream, horseradish, and green pepper or pimiento. Simmer about 5 minutes. Serve on buns. Makes about 3 cups.

SOUPERBURGERS

1 pound ground beef
½ cup chopped onion
1 can (10¾ ounces) condensed
chicken gumbo, cream of
mushroom, golden mushroom, or
tomato soup
1 tablespoon prepared mustard
6 buns, split and toasted

In skillet, brown beef and cook onion until tender (use shortening if necessary); stir to separate meat. Add soup and seasonings; simmer 5 to 10 minutes to blend flavors. Stir often. Serve on buns. Makes about 3 cups.

PIZZABURGER

1 pound ground beef
¼ cup chopped onion
1 can (10¾ ounces) condensed
tomato soup
½ cup shredded sharp cheese
⅛ teaspoon oregano
Dash pepper
8 buns, split and toasted

In skillet, brown beef and cook onion until tender (use shortening if necessary); stir to separate meat. Add soup, cheese, oregano, and pepper. Simmer about 10 minutes. Serve on buns. Makes about 3 cups.

WESTERN STYLE SANDWICH

1 can (11¼ ounces) condensed
chili beef soup
¼ cup water
4 slices toast
4 slices tomato
4 thin slices onion
4 slices mild process cheese,
cut into strips

Blend soup and water. Spread on toast; *cover edges completely*. Broil 4 inches from heat for 5 minutes. Top with tomato, onion, and cheese. Broil until cheese melts. Makes 4 open-face sandwiches.

CALIFORNIA OPEN-FACE

8 slices bacon
1 can (11 ounces) condensed
Cheddar cheese soup
⅓ cup milk
1 teaspoon lemon juice
Dash cayenne pepper
2 medium tomatoes, sliced
4 slices toast, buttered

Cook bacon until crisp; pour off drippings. Set aside. Stir soup into skillet. Add milk, lemon juice, and pepper; blend until smooth. Heat slowly; stir often. Meanwhile, make open-face sandwiches by placing tomatoes and bacon on toast; pour hot sauce over. Makes 8 open-face sandwiches.

FRANK AND BEAN SANDWICH

6 frankfurters
¼ cup chopped onion
2 tablespoons butter or margarine
1 can (11½ ounces) condensed
  bean with bacon soup
¼ cup water
¼ cup ketchup
¼ cup sweet pickle relish
6 frankfurter buns, slit and toasted

In skillet, brown frankfurters and cook onion in butter until tender. Add remaining ingredients except buns. Heat; stir occasionally. Serve frankfurters on buns with sauce. Makes 6 sandwiches.

SHRIMP-CRAB BISQUE SANDWICHES

1 can (10¾ ounces) condensed
  cream of mushroom soup
1 cup cooked crab meat, flaked
1 cup diced cooked shrimp
¼ cup finely chopped celery
¼ cup finely chopped onion
½ teaspoon lemon juice
¼ teaspoon Worcestershire
6 slices toast or rusks
3 slices (about 3 ounces) Swiss
  cheese, cut in half
⅓ cup milk
¼ cup finely chopped green pepper

Combine ¼ cup soup, crab, shrimp, celery, onion, lemon juice, and Worcestershire. Spread mixture evenly over toast; *cover edges completely.* Top with cheese. Broil 4 inches from heat for 5 minutes or until hot and cheese melts. Meanwhile, in saucepan, combine remaining soup, milk, and green pepper. Heat; stir occasionally. Serve over toast. Makes 6 open-face sandwiches.

PUMPERNICKEL-KRAUT FRANKS

1 can (11½ ounces) condensed
  bean with bacon soup
4 slices pumpernickel bread,
  lightly toasted
1½ cups sauerkraut, drained
4 frankfurters, slit lengthwise
¼ cup ketchup

Spread soup on bread; cover with sauerkraut. Top each sandwich with a frankfurter; spread with ketchup. Broil until sandwiches are hot, about 8 minutes. Makes 4 open-face sandwiches.

CHICKEN SPREAD-A-BURGER

1 can (10¾ ounces) condensed
  cream of chicken soup
1 cup diced cooked chicken
¼ cup finely chopped celery
2 tablespoons finely chopped onion
2 tablespoons chopped pimiento
Dash pepper
4 frankfurter buns, split and
  toasted

Combine soup, chicken, celery, onion, pimiento, and pepper. Spread mixture evenly over bun halves; *cover edges completely.* Broil about 4 inches from heat until hot, about 7 minutes. 4 open-face sandwiches.

CANTONESE CHICKEN SANDWICH

½ medium onion, sliced
1 tablespoon butter or margarine
1 can (10¾ ounces) condensed
  cream of chicken soup
⅓ cup milk
¼ cup sliced water chestnuts
1 tablespoon soy sauce
4 servings sliced cooked chicken
  or turkey
4 slices buttered toast

In saucepan, cook onion in butter until onion is just tender. Stir in soup, milk, water chestnuts, and soy sauce. Heat; stir often. Arrange chicken on toast; pour sauce over. Makes 4 open-face sandwiches.

CHINA BOY SANDWICH

1 can (10¾ ounces) condensed
  cream of mushroom soup
1 cup diced cooked chicken
¼ cup thinly sliced celery
¼ cup sliced water chestnuts
¼ cup chopped onion
1 teaspoon soy sauce
4 frankfurter buns, split and toasted

Combine soup, chicken, celery, water chestnuts, onion, and soy sauce. Spread mixture evenly over bun halves; *cover edges completely.* Broil about 4 inches from heat until hot, about 7 minutes. 4 open-face sandwiches.

SAUCY QUICK SANDWICH

4 servings sliced cooked ham or
  chicken
4 slices toast
1 package (10 ounces) frozen
  asparagus spears, cooked and
  drained
1 can (10¾ ounces) condensed
  cream of celery, chicken,
  mushroom, or Cheddar cheese
  soup
¼ to ⅓ cup milk

Place chicken on toast; top with
asparagus. In saucepan, combine
soup and milk. Heat; stir occasionally. Pour sauce over sandwiches.
Makes 4 open-face sandwiches.

BARBECUED STEAK SANDWICH

1 pound boneless sirloin steak
  (¾" thick)
¼ cup chopped onion
1 large clove garlic, minced
1 teaspoon barbecue seasoning
2 tablespoons butter or margarine
1 can (10¾ ounces) condensed
  tomato soup
¼ cup water
Long hard rolls or frankfurter buns,
  split and toasted

Freeze meat 1 hour to firm (makes
slicing easier); slice into *very thin*
strips. In skillet, cook onion with
garlic and seasoning in butter until
just tender; push to one side. Add
meat; cook until color changes
(about 3 to 4 minutes). Add soup
and water. Heat; stir occasionally.
Serve in buns. Makes about 2½
cups.

BRUNCH PANCAKE SANDWICH

4 slices bacon
1 can (10¾ ounces) condensed
  cream of mushroom soup
½ cup milk
4 hard-cooked eggs, sliced
2 tablespoons chopped pimiento
Pancakes

In saucepan, cook bacon until crisp;
remove and crumble. Pour off fat.
Stir in soup; gradually blend in
milk. Add bacon, eggs, and pimiento. Heat; stir occasionally. Alternate
pancakes and creamed eggs. Makes
about 2½ cups.

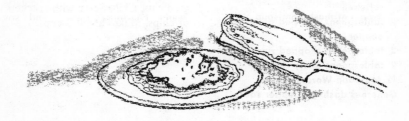

Dips and Spreads

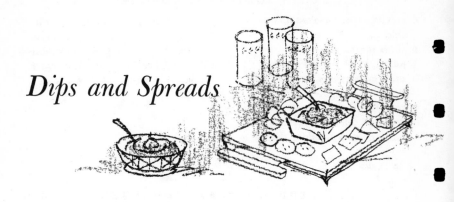

When company is coming or refrigerator-raiders descend, dips made with soup are creamy smooth, extra tasty, and extra easy. Take a can of hearty black bean soup and let it form the basis for a zesty, welcoming dip . . . or choose tangy tomato soup or peppy bean with bacon soup.

Whatever your favorites, you'll enjoy teaming soup dips with assorted crackers, potato chips, pretzels, and other "dunkable munchables." For a vitamin-packed change, try using crisp carrot sticks, celery sticks, or cauliflowerets for dunking. Or let the dip double as a spread for sandwiches and hors d' oeuvres.

You can match your dip to the mood of the occasion when you choose from the variety provided by flavorful condensed soups. Just let your imagination take over.

SPANISH DIP

1 can (10¾ ounces) condensed cream of celery soup
1 package (8 ounces) cream cheese, softened
2 tablespoons chopped green pepper
2 tablespoons chopped ripe olives
2 tablespoons finely chopped onion
¼ teaspoon Worcestershire
Generous dash hot pepper sauce

With electric mixer or rotary beater, gradually blend soup into cream cheese. Add remaining ingredients. Chill. Serve with crackers or chips. Makes about 2 cups.

DILLED DIP

1 can (10¾ ounces) condensed
   cream of celery soup
1 package (8 ounces) cream cheese,
   softened
½ cup chopped cucumber
2 tablespoons finely chopped onion
¼ teaspoon dried dill leaves,
   crushed
⅛ teaspoon hot pepper sauce

With electric mixer or rotary beater, gradually blend soup into cream cheese. Add cucumber, onion, dill, and pepper sauce. Chill. Serve with crackers or chips. Makes about 2 cups.

NEW ENGLANDER'S SPECIAL

1 can (10¾ ounces) condensed
   New England clam chowder soup
¼ cup chili sauce
2 tablespoons finely chopped onion
1 package (8 ounces) cream cheese,
   softened

With electric mixer or rotary beater, gradually blend soup, chili sauce, and onion into cream cheese. Chill. Serve with crackers or chips. Makes about 2½ cups.

SHRIMP BLUE CHEESE DIP

1 can (11 ounces) condensed
   Cheddar cheese soup
2 tablespoons crumbled blue cheese
1 tablespoon finely chopped onion
1 teaspoon sherry
⅛ teaspoon hot pepper sauce
1 package (8 ounces) cream cheese,
   softened
Cooked shrimp

With electric mixer or rotary beater, gradually blend soup, blue cheese, onion, sherry, and hot pepper sauce into cream cheese. Chill. Serve with shrimp, crackers, or chips. Makes about 2 cups.

ZIPPY BEAN DUNK

1 package (8 ounces) cream cheese,
   softened
1 can (11 ounces) condensed
   black bean soup
2 tablespoons grated onion
Dash hot pepper sauce
Dash garlic powder

Beat cream cheese with rotary beater or electric mixer until smooth. Gradually add remaining ingredients; blend thoroughly. Chill. Makes about 2 cups.

CLAM DIGGERS DUNK

1 can (10¾ ounces) condensed
   New England clam chowder soup
1 package (8 ounces) cream cheese,
   softened
1 can (4 ounces) mushrooms,
   drained and chopped
1 tablespoon finely chopped onion
Dash cayenne pepper

With rotary beater or slow speed of electric mixer, gradually blend soup into cream cheese. Add remaining ingredients. Chill. Serve with crackers or chips. Makes about 2½ cups.

BACON 'N BEAN DIP

1 can (11½ ounces) condensed
   bean with bacon soup
¼ cup chili sauce
2 tablespoons minced green pepper,
   if desired
1 teaspoon minced onion
1 teaspoon Worcestershire

Mix all ingredients; chill. Especially tasty with bacon wafers. If smoother dip is desired, beat in electric mixer or blender. May also be used as a sandwich spread, served on toast. Makes about 1½ cups.

CAPE COD DIP

1 can (10¾ ounces) condensed
   New England clam chowder soup
1 medium clove garlic, minced
½ teaspoon Worcestershire
1 package (8 ounces) cream cheese,
   softened

With electric mixer or rotary beater, gradually blend soup, garlic, and Worcestershire into cream cheese; beat until just smooth. Chill. Serve with crackers or chips. Makes about 2 cups.

DEVILED DELIGHT

1 package (8 ounces) cream cheese,
   softened
1 can (10¾ ounces) condensed
   tomato soup
2 cans (4½ ounces each) deviled
   ham
¼ cup finely chopped cucumber
2 teaspoons finely chopped green
   onion
1 small clove garlic, minced

Beat cream cheese until smooth with electric mixer or rotary beater. Add remaining ingredients; blend thoroughly. Chill. Makes about 2 cups. Serve as dip or spread for crackers, Melba toast, buttered bread.

Soups and the Freezer

Your freezer can be a real friend when unexpected company pops in or when your schedule's extra tight. It's so nice to know that your tasty homemade specialties are just waiting on the freezer shelf, ready to help you maintain your culinary reputation at a moment's notice. You can cut down on last-minute dinner party preparation time, too, if you make the main dish ahead of time and freeze it. It's fun to be the unruffled hostess and still come through with a delightful meal.

If frozen properly, your food will retain every bit of the fresh taste and bright color you enjoy so much. Just remember to package your food in air and moisture-proof wrappers and containers, and to keep your freezer set at 0°F. or lower.

It's also a good idea to organize the packages in your freezer so you can find each item of food when you want it. One way is to post a list near the freezer and write down each item as you store it, checking it off when you remove it for use. This way you'll know exactly what foods you have for planning nutritious, interesting meals.

Soups contribute a great deal to households with freezers by helping with the preparation of special cooked dishes. If you're the lucky owner of a freezer, you know it's as easy to prepare a double amount of foods that freeze well—part to be eaten at once and part to be frozen. Many casseroles lend themselves especially well to this—and by using a can of soup for sauce, you can halve your cooking time. This is true also for creamed chicken and similar dishes to be frozen.

Research has shown that meats particularly freeze better when prepared with a sauce; this protects the meat from contact with air—and, therefore, aids in preventing off-flavors. Soup sauces are especially good for freezing because they retain their smooth consistency at low temperatures.

Other pointers to insure good results in freezing prepared foods are these:

1. Freeze only as much of a prepared food as you can use in one month or soon after. Generally, a fairly fast turnover is recommended by freezer specialists—rather than long storage of any food items.

2. Cool a cooked food as fast as possible and wrap it carefully so it is moistureproof.

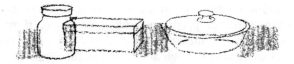

3. For packaging, you may place mixture in plastic freezer container or glass jar; leave 1-inch of head space at top because food will expand when frozen. Another method is to freeze and store the casserole mixture or similar food right in the casserole if you have one to spare. Or line a clean casserole with heavy duty aluminum foil, enough to wrap completely around the food and seal over the top. Pour in the food and seal foil with a double fold (press down tight against food). Place casserole in freezer until food is frozen solid. Then simply remove the foil-wrapped frozen food from the casserole . . . it will keep its shape and be protected in the freezer. When ready to serve the dish, remove it from foil (still frozen); put in pan to heat.

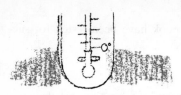

4. Freezing at 0°F. or lower is important to success with any kind of food. Put unfrozen foods in the fastest freezing area or in direct contact with freezer walls or shelves and away from already frozen foods. Place packages so air can circulate among them. Do not overload freezer with a large number of foods to be frozen at once.

5. Label each package with date, name of product, and number of servings.

6. Freeze in one package an average amount for serving your family. Large amounts take a long time to freeze—and to heat later on for serving (unless thawed completely before re-heating). Food in a large casserole may burn around the edges before it is warm in the center.

7. When preparing casseroles or stews for freezing, shorten cooking time slightly to allow for the additional cooking which takes place during re-heating.

8. To prepare a frozen main dish for serving, you may thaw it in the refrigerator—and bake as usual as soon as thawed. Or you may heat the frozen item in the oven—allowing longer heating time than specified in the original recipe (you will need to check dish during baking since no specific rule for increased baking time can be given for all dishes).

A number of dishes throughout this book have been tested for successful freezing. These include (see index):

Macaroni and Cheese—Family Style
Old Fashioned Meat Loaf (leave off topping)
Tomato Beef Stew (do not flour meat; leave out potatoes and thyme)

The following recipes also freeze well:

MUSHROOM STROGANOFF

1 pound boneless round steak
    (¾" thick)
½ cup chopped onion
2 tablespoons butter or margarine
1 can (10¾ ounces) condensed
    cream of mushroom or
    golden mushroom soup
½ cup sour cream
¼ cup water
½ teaspoon paprika
Cooked noodles

Freeze meat 1 hour to firm (makes slicing easier); slice into *very* thin strips. In skillet, cook onion in butter until *just* tender; push to one side. Add meat; cook until color *just* changes (about 3 to 4 minutes). Add remaining ingredients except noodles. Heat; stir occasionally. Serve over noodles. Makes about 3½ cups.

To freeze: add ⅓ cup water to beef mixture after cooking. Pour into a 1-quart casserole. Store in freezer. To reheat, do not preheat oven. Bake covered at 450°F. for 45 minutes or until hot; stir.

CHILI MEATBALLS

1 pound ground beef
¼ cup fine dry bread crumbs
¼ cup finely chopped onion
1 egg, slightly beaten
2 teaspoons chili powder
¼ teaspoon salt
1 can (10¾ ounces) condensed
    tomato soup
2 tablespoons water
Cooked rice

Mix thoroughly beef, crumbs, onion, egg, 1 teaspoon chili powder, and salt; shape into 16 meatballs. In skillet, brown meatballs (use shortening if necessary); pour off fat. Stir in soup, water, and remaining chili powder. Cover; cook over low heat 20 minutes. Stir occasionally. Serve with rice. Makes about 3 cups.

To freeze: Add ½ cup water to meatball mixture after cooking. Pour into a 1-quart casserole. Store in freezer. To reheat, do not preheat oven. Bake at 450°F. for 45 minutes or until hot; stir.

All
About
Soups

What a difference soup makes! This food of many faces has delighted tastebuds, satisfied hunger, and perked up appetites from the beginning of time.

Today, condensed and ready-to-serve soups enhance tradition yet spark fresh new ideas. Try a bowlful as a breakfast-brightener. Spruce-up snacktime with a cheery cupful. Send it in a lunch box for that note of warmth. Dress it up for a party. Whatever your choice, a wonderful variety of soups is as handy as your cupboard for enjoyment 'round the clock, 'round the year.

Contemporary soup service is the subject of the following chapters.

Nourishing Soup
Through the Day

Breakfast through supper, soup scores high in creative menu-planning. Let these suggestions serve as a springboard for other enterprising ideas.

1. EMBELLISH THAT BREAKFAST: Climb out of the cereal rut and join the soup-for-breakfast people. A bowl of condensed beef soup with its nubbins of barley, bright vegetables, and meat pieces could be just the interesting change needed to make the morning meal fun again.

WARM-UP BREAKFAST
Sliced Orange
Bowl of Beef Soup
Toast and Jelly
Crisp Bacon Curls
Milk

SUNNY STARTER
Grapefruit Sections
French Toast
Mug of Tomato Soup
   (made with milk)

2. MILK-MINDERS: When it seems harder and harder to convince your brood to drink milk with meals, it's time to resort to more subtle ways. Soups are one answer. Many condensed soups can be heated with milk instead of water; skim milk or non-fat dry milk fill dieters' needs.

MILK BONUS SNACKS
Cream of Mushroom Mug
Peanut Butter Crackers
   . . .
Cream of Tomato Cup
Cinnamon Toast

ANY DAY DINNER
Cream of Potato Soup
Ham Steak   Green Beans
Salad with Russian Dressing
Italian Bread
Apple Strudel   Sliced Cheese

3. VEGETABLES INCOGNITO: Some folks would rather sip their vegetables than spear them. Vegetable and vegetable-based soups are just right.

LUNCH BOX WINNER
Minestrone (in vacuum bottle)
Tuna Fish Sandwich
Brownies   Fruit
Milk

SUPPER SPECIAL
Chunky Vegetable Soup
Barbecued Frankfurters
Toasted Buns   Fresh Fruit Salad
Cookies   Milk

4. MAKE MINE MEATLESS: If meals without meat are part of your future, count on soup to add interest, variety—as appetizers, main dishes, and cooking ingredients. Look for the following meatless kinds:

PENNYWISE DINNER
Purée Mongole*
Saucy Fish Fillets*
Baked Potatoes   Buttered Broccoli
Berries in Patty Shells   Cream

OVEN SUPPER
Clam Chowder
Tuna Noodle Casserole*
Baked Stuffed Tomatoes
Spice Cake

5. THE PAUSE THAT NOURISHES: Everyone loves a work break. Whether the activity is cleaning the attic or programing computers, it goes faster after a pick-me-up, especially one that's nourishing as well as tasty. That's the beauty of soup. So many kinds. Hot and cold. Invigorating. Some, like beef broth and consommé, are low-calorie, too.

6. SOUPER SNACKS: Soup says "welcome home" to kids after school . . . vegetable and green pea are tops. Soup assures happy midnight feasting for movie buffs . . . how about onion? Soup makes a good travel companion . . . pack chicken noodle and vegetable beef. And soup is the perfect nightcap to bring tranquil dreams . . . enjoy cream of chicken or chicken with rice.

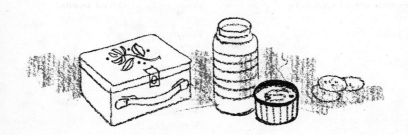

PLANNING BALANCED MENUS

Planning makes the difference—between hit-or-miss nutrition and meals that have what it takes for good health.

The great variety of soups available—from clear broths to hearty chowders—can be helpful in making balanced menus. Here's how they fit into the Four Food Groups.*

1. MILK GROUP:	2. MEAT GROUP:	3. VEGETABLE-FRUIT GROUP:	4. BREAD-CEREAL GROUP:
Cheddar Cheese	Bean with Bacon	Bisque of Tomato	Beef Noodle
New England Clam Chowder	Beef	Chicken Vegetable	Chicken 'n Dumplings
Oyster Stew	Black Bean	Chunky Beef	Chicken & Stars
Potato, Cream of	Chili Beef	Chunky Clam Chowder	Chicken Noodle-O's
Shrimp, Cream of	Chunky Beef	Chunky Sirloin Burger	Chunky Chicken
	Chunky Chicken	Chunky Turkey	Curly Noodle
	Chunky Sirloin Burger	Chunky Vegetable	Golden Vegetable Noodle-O's
	Chunky Turkey	Clam Chowder (Manhattan Style)	Noodles & Ground Beef
	Green Pea		Tomato-Beef Noodle-O's
	Hot Dog Bean	Golden Vegetable Noodle-O's	Turkey Noodle
	Split Pea with Ham	Minestrone	
		Old Fashioned Tomato Rice	
		Old Fashioned Vegetable	
		Scotch Broth	
		Stockpot	
		Tomato	
		Turkey Vegetable	
		Vegetable	
		Vegetable Beef	
		Vegetarian Vegetable	

*See page 4.

Top 'o the Morning

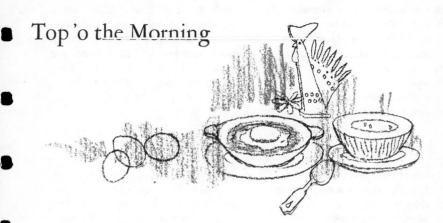

Those who know the joys of soup for breakfast—hearty, warming, invigorating—boast about their eye-openers. Steaming from bowl or mug, soup takes to the table with genuine ease—perhaps with a generous pat of butter melting on top. Joined by crisp toast or muffins, bacon or sausage, fruit, and milk, soup helps start the day with a smile.

Soup gives bonus flavor to the usual breakfast foods, too. Try eggs poached in soup for a lively innovation, or eggs scrambled with one of the cream soups, or dried beef creamed in a soup sauce. Seconds, please!

COLD DAY BREAKFAST
Grapefruit Half
Green Pea Soup
Coffee Cake
Cocoa

SPRING DAY BREAKFAST
Fruit in Season
Savory Poached Eggs*
   on English Muffins
Milk or Coffee

SUMMER BREAKFAST
Half Cantaloupe
Tomato Soup (made with milk)
   with Corn Flakes on top
Buttered Toast   Ham
Milk or Coffee

AUTUMN BREAKFAST
Orange Sections
Vegetable Beef Soup
Date Nut Bread
Milk or Coffee

SAVORY POACHED EGGS

2 tablespoons butter or margarine
1 can (10¾ ounces) condensed
   cream of celery, chicken, or
   mushroom soup
½ cup milk
6 eggs
3 English muffins (split, toasted,
   and buttered)

Melt butter in heavy skillet. Blend in soup and milk; heat to boiling. Gently slip eggs into soup sauce; cook over low heat until whites are firm. Place eggs on muffins. Pour sauce over eggs. 6 servings.

CAMPBELLED EGGS

1 can (11 ounces) condensed
   Cheddar cheese, cream of celery,
   chicken, or mushroom soup
8 eggs, slightly beaten
Dash pepper
2 tablespoons butter or margarine

In bowl, stir soup until smooth; gradually blend in eggs and pepper. In 10-inch skillet, melt butter; pour in egg mixture. Cook over low heat. As mixture begins to set around edges, gently lift cooked portions with large turner so that thin, uncooked portion can flow to the bottom. Continue gently lifting cooked portions until eggs are completely set, but still moist. 4 servings.

CREAMED DRIED BEEF

¼ cup chopped onion
2 tablespoons butter or margarine
1 can (10¾ ounces) condensed
   cream of mushroom soup
½ cup milk
1 package (4 ounces) sliced
   dried beef, rinsed
Toast

In saucepan, cook onion in butter until tender. Stir in soup, milk, and beef. Heat; stir occasionally. Serve over toast. Makes about 2 cups.

DON FAR TONG *(Egg Drop Soup)*

2 cans (10½ ounces each)
   condensed beef broth
2 soup cans water
1 cup cooked peas
¼ cup thinly sliced green onions
1 teaspoon soy sauce
1 egg, slightly beaten

In saucepan, combine all ingredients except egg. Bring to boil. Gradually pour egg into simmering soup, stirring gently until egg is set. Serve immediately. Makes about 5 cups.

Campbelled Eggs   Page 132

Magic Menu Maker
for Lunches
and
Lunch Box Meals

The American way of lunch—soup and sandwiches. What a great way to include vegetables, meat, or milk in noon meals.

Here are some tips to help you pack the best lunches ever:

1. Plan a well-balanced meal with a few extras to satisfy your "luncher." Select favorite foods and food combinations—one of the best is soup and sandwiches. An occasional "surprise" would be a welcome treat. Plenty of paper napkins and colorful straws for sipping milk are other "inviting" touches for the lunch box.

2. For sandwiches, use a variety of fillings and breads. If you make up sandwiches the night before they're to be eaten, keep them refrigerated until you pack the lunch. Wrap sandwiches in moistureproof, clear lunch box wrap material or foil as soon as they are made.

3. Wrap lettuce or other moist fillings, such as sliced tomatoes, separately. Do not include salad-type meat fillings for sandwiches unless the lunch can be stored in a cool place—and will only be held for a short time.

4. Always have one hot dish. You're sure of pleasing if you include a vacuum bottle of hot soup. Any of the condensed and ready to serve soups are good to carry. And many kinds may be prepared with milk —nutritional plus. A wide-mouth vacuum bottle is ideal for soup— easy to pour into and to eat from. Make sure the soup's hot before packing (rinse the vacuum bottle with hot water before pouring in soup). Be sure to send along a soup spoon or a long-handled spoon for eating right from the bottle.

Soup Mate—Chicken Vegetable and Golden Vegetable Noodle-O's, Frankfurter

Split Pea with Ham Soup Served with Chopped Tomato, Ham and Cheese Sandwich

135

GREAT EATING AT HOME OR AWAY—

SOUPS	SANDWICHES	DESSERTS	TIPS FOR LUNCH BOX
Cream of Asparagus	Meat loaf on hard roll	Fig bars	Cut sandwich roll in half for easy eating
Bean with Bacon	Sliced ham and lettuce on rye bread	Apple	Wrap lettuce for sandwich in waxed paper
Beef	Swiss cheese on whole wheat bread	Peaches (fresh or canned)	Pack cole slaw in container with lid
Beef Noodle	Liverwurst and onion on white	Cherry strudel	Pack celery and carrot sticks
Black Bean	Tomato and bacon on whole wheat bread	Pineapple (fresh or canned)	Spread bread with butter—prevents moist filling from soaking into bread
Chunky Beef	Sharp cheese and lettuce on white bread	Fruit tapioca	Pack a plastic fork or spoon
Cream of Celery	Salmon salad and lettuce on hard roll	Blueberry pie tart	Pack a few cherry tomatoes
Cream of Chicken	Ham and cheese— "double decker"	Grapes and oatmeal cookies	Use white and dark bread
Cream of Potato	Corned beef on rye	Fruit cocktail Molasses Cookies	Pack cole slaw
Chicken Gumbo	Cream cheese and ham on date-nut bread	Orange	Peel and section orange; pack in sandwich bag
Chicken Noodle	Egg, bacon, and lettuce on whole wheat bread	Apple sauce cake	Add radishes or green pepper for crunch
Chicken with Rice	Salami, tomato, cheese on roll	Chocolate chip cookies	Use clear plastic wrap for sandwiches
Chunky Chicken	Peanut butter and jelly on white bread	Sliced peaches	Pack celery sticks
Chili Beef	Sliced cheese on hard sesame roll	Banana	Put in lettuce for sandwich and carrot sticks for nibbling
Clam Chowder	Egg salad on pumpernickel bread	Cherries (fresh or canned)	Pickles and olives go well with sandwich

WITH SOUP AS A TASTY STARTER

SOUPS	SANDWICHES	DESSERTS	TIPS FOR LUNCH BOX
Chicken & Stars	Bologna, cheese, lettuce on white bread	Tomato soup cake	Add a small bag of salted nuts
Green Pea	Ham salad on poppyseed roll	Apricots (fresh or canned)	Keep vacuum bottle clean and "sweet"— rinse with baking soda solution
Minestrone	Sliced chicken on hard roll	Orange sections	Freeze sandwiches for lunch boxes
Cream of Mushroom	Roast beef on rye bread	Banana	Wrap crisp vegetables to munch
Pepper Pot	Cream cheese and dried beef on white bread	Pears (fresh or canned)	Use glass jars with tops for desserts
Scotch Broth	Luncheon loaf on rye bread	Sliced Peaches	Tuck in a small box of raisins
Split Pea with Ham	Chicken spread and stuffed olives on roll	Fruit cocktail	Put in lettuce for sandwich
Tomato	Tuna salad on hard roll	Chocolate cup cake	Pack some green grapes
Tomato Rice	Roast beef on white bread	Baked apple	Be sure to include a napkin or two
Turkey Noodle	Deviled ham and tomato on whole wheat bread	Lemon pie tart	Wrap slices of tomato in foil for sandwich
Turkey Vegetable	Sliced ham and cheese on rye	Butterscotch pudding	Pack cole slaw
Vegetable	Bacon, lettuce, sliced tomato on soft roll	Brownies	Wrap sandwich items separately—let "luncher" put together
Vegetable Beef	Cream cheese and olive on brown bread	Plums (fresh or canned)	Include a hard-cooked egg
Vegetarian Vegetable	Sliced turkey, lettuce on club roll	Applesauce, Gingerbread	Put mayonnaise in small piece of foil

137

Souper Soups

Here come the heartiest, happiest, homiest soups of them all . . . the Souper Soups! Chock-full of stick-to-the-ribs goodness, these robust soups will turn an after-the-game snack into a feast, or get a light meal off to a rip-roaring start. And each has a distinct personality . . . one or more condensed soups serve as a base for a variety of substantial and savory additions. M'm! M'm! Good!

SOUPER SOUP MENUS

Rosy Chili and Beef Soup*
Chef Salad   Corn Muffins
Blueberry Turnovers (frozen)

Chicken Pea Soup Bowl*
Fruit Salad   Rolls
Coconut Custard Pie

Seafood and Tomato Bowl*
Crackers   Cheese
Deviled Eggs   Relishes
Apple Pie Tarts (frozen)

Italian Bowl*
Antipasta
Toasted Italian Bread
Spumoni

ROSY CHILI AND BEEF SOUP

½ **pound ground beef**
2 **tablespoons chopped onion**
1 **teaspoon chili powder**
½ **teaspoon salt**
1 **tablespoon butter or margarine**
1 **can (10¾ ounces) condensed tomato soup**
1 **can (11 ounces) condensed beef soup**
1½ **soup cans water**

Combine beef, onion, chili powder, and salt; shape into 12 small meatballs. In saucepan, brown meatballs in butter. Add soups and water. Heat; stir often. Makes about 4 cups.

OLD FASHIONED VEGETABLE-BACON SOUP

3 slices bacon
¼ cup green pepper strips
⅛ teaspoon tarragon leaves,
 crushed
1 can (10½ ounces) condensed
 old fashioned vegetable soup
1 soup can water

In saucepan, cook bacon until crisp; remove and crumble. Pour off all but 1 tablespoon drippings. Cook green pepper with tarragon in drippings until tender. Add soup and water. Heat; stir occasionally. Garnish with bacon. Makes about 2½ cups.

SWISS POTATO SOUP

1 can (10¾ ounces) condensed
 cream of potato soup
⅛ teaspoon dry mustard
1 soup can milk
½ cup shredded Swiss cheese
2 tablespoons chopped parsley

In saucepan, blend soup and mustard. Add milk, cheese, and parsley. Heat until cheese melts. Stir occasionally. Makes about 2½ cups.

HEARTY FRANKFURTER SOUP

2 frankfurters, thinly sliced
2 tablespoons chopped onion
1 tablespoon butter or margarine
1 can (11 ounces) condensed
 tomato rice soup
1 soup can water

Brown frankfurters and onion in butter. Add soup and water. Heat; stir often. Makes about 2½ cups.

CREAMY SALMON SOUP

½ cup chopped cucumber
2 tablespoons chopped onion
⅛ teaspoon dried dill leaves,
 crushed
1 tablespoon butter or margarine
1 can (10¾ ounces) condensed
 cream of celery soup
⅓ cup sour cream
1 cup water
1 can (8 ounces) salmon, drained
 and flaked

In saucepan, cook cucumber and onion with dill in butter until tender. Blend in soup and sour cream; gradually add water and salmon. Heat; stir occasionally. Makes about 4 cups.

COUNTRY WARMER

1 can (10½ ounces) condensed
chicken vegetable soup
1 soup can milk
1 cup cooked lima beans
4 slices bacon, cooked and
crumbled

In saucepan, combine soup, milk, and lima beans. Heat; stir occasionally. Garnish with bacon. Makes about 3 cups.

TUNA POTATO CHOWDER

2 slices bacon
¼ cup chopped onion
2 tablespoons chopped green
pepper
1 can (10¾ ounces) condensed
cream of potato soup
½ soup can milk
½ soup can water
1 can (about 7 ounces) tuna,
drained and flaked
Dash mace

In saucepan, cook bacon until crisp; remove and crumble. Pour off all but 2 tablespoons drippings. Cook onion and green pepper in drippings until tender. Add remaining ingredients. Heat; stir occasionally. Garnish with bacon. Makes about 3 cups.

PANHANDLE POTPOURRI

½ cup chopped onion
2 tablespoons butter or margarine
1 can (10¾ ounces) condensed
cream of celery soup
1 can (10¾ ounces) condensed
cream of mushroom soup
1 can (10¾ ounces) condensed
chicken noodle soup
1 soup can milk
1 soup can water
1 package (4 ounces) sliced dried
beef, rinsed and chopped
1 package (10 ounces) frozen
succotash, cooked and drained
Dash pepper

In large saucepan, cook onion in butter until tender. Blend in soups; gradually stir in remaining ingredients. Heat; stir occasionally. Makes about 8½ cups.

DEEP SEA SIPPER

¼ cup chopped onion
Dash crushed thyme leaves
1 tablespoon butter or margarine
1 can (10¾ ounces) condensed
  cream of shrimp soup
1 soup can milk
1 cup flaked cooked white fish
½ cup cooked cut green beans

In saucepan, cook onion with thyme in butter until tender. Add remaining ingredients. Heat; stir occasionally. Makes about 4 cups.

SPLIT PEA 'N TOMATO

1 can (11½ ounces) condensed
  split pea with ham soup
1 can (10¾ ounces) condensed
  tomato soup
1 cup milk
1 cup water

In saucepan, blend soups. Gradually stir in milk and water. Heat; stir often. Makes about 4½ cups.

BURGOO SOUP

1 small onion, sliced
⅛ teaspoon nutmeg
2 tablespoons butter or margarine
1 can (10¾ ounces) condensed
  cream of chicken soup
1 can (11¼ ounces) condensed
  green pea soup
1 can (5 ounces) boned chicken or
  turkey, or 1 cup diced cooked
  chicken or turkey
1 cup cooked sliced carrots
1 cup chopped spinach
1½ soup cans water

In saucepan, cook onion and nutmeg in butter until onion is tender. Add remaining ingredients. Cover; simmer 5 minutes; stir often. Makes about 5½ cups.

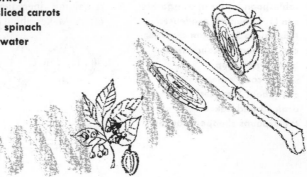

SOUP PLUS

A pattern recipe to use as you like with foods you have on hand.

½ cup cooked meat or poultry,
   cut in strips
1 tablespoon butter or margarine
1 can any Campbell's Soup
1 soup can milk or water
½ cup cooked vegetables

In saucepan, cook meat in butter until lightly browned. Add remaining ingredients. Heat; stir often. Makes about 2½ cups.

CHUNKY CHICKEN PARMESAN

1 can (19 ounces) chunky
   chicken soup
¼ cup grated Parmesan cheese
2 tablespoons chopped parsley

In saucepan, combine all ingredients. Heat; stir occasionally. Makes about 2 cups.

ITALIAN BOWL

½ pound link sausage,
   cut into small pieces
2 cans (10½ ounces each)
   condensed minestrone soup
1 can (10¾ ounces) condensed
   tomato soup
3 soup cans water
Croutons

In saucepan, cook sausage until done. Pour off fat. Add soups and water. Heat; stir occasionally. Top with croutons. Makes about 7½ cups.

MOBY SOUP

¼ cup chopped onion
1 small clove garlic, minced
1 tablespoon butter or margarine
1 can (10¾ ounces) condensed
   Manhattan Style clam chowder
1 can (11 ounces) condensed
   tomato rice soup
1½ soup cans water
1 can (about 7 ounces) tuna,
   drained and flaked
2 tablespoons chopped parsley

In saucepan, cook onion and garlic in butter until onion is tender. Add remaining ingredients. Heat; stir often. Makes about 5 cups.

SAUSAGE MINESTRONE

3 sausage links, sliced
1 can (10½ ounces) condensed
   minestrone soup
1 soup can water

In saucepan, cook sausage until done; pour off fat. Add soup and water. Heat; stir occasionally. Makes about 2½ cups.

CHICKEN CORN CHOWDER

1 can (10¾ ounces) condensed
   cream of chicken soup
2 soup cans milk
1 can (10¾ ounces) condensed
   chicken noodle soup
1 can (16 ounces) cream style corn
1 can (5 ounces) boned chicken, or
   1 cup diced cooked chicken

In saucepan, blend cream of chicken soup and milk. Add remaining ingredients. Heat; stir occasionally. Makes about 7 cups.

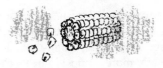

PATCHWORK KETTLE

¼ cup chopped onion
⅛ teaspoon ground sage
1 tablespoon butter or margarine
1 can (10¾ ounces) condensed
   cream of chicken soup
1 can (10½ ounces) condensed
   vegetarian vegetable soup
1 soup can water
½ soup can milk
½ cup Canadian bacon cut in
   thin strips
½ cup chopped cooked spinach

In saucepan, cook onion with sage in butter until tender. Blend in remaining ingredients. Heat; stir occasionally. Makes about 5½ cups.

FRANK AND BEAN SOUP

½ pound frankfurters, thinly sliced
2 tablespoons butter or margarine
1 can (11½ ounces) condensed
   bean with bacon soup
1 can (11¼ ounces) condensed
   green pea soup
2 soup cans water

In saucepan, brown frankfurters in butter. Blend in soups; gradually stir in water. Heat; stir occasionally. Makes about 6 cups.

Youngsters Like Soup

Kids love soup! And it's no wonder. So many kinds to choose from spells mealtime satisfaction for each and every child. Soup is ideal for lunchboxes, snacks, camp-outs, and cook-outs.

What's more, soup is fun to eat. Try the following suggestions and see.

"GROWING-UP" SOUPS may be given to your baby when he's ready for soft chewing foods. Some recommended by doctors include: cream of asparagus, cream of celery, beef, beef noodle, chicken noodle, chicken with rice, green pea, Scotch broth, tomato, vegetable, vegetable beef, vegetarian vegetable, chicken vegetable, and turkey noodle.

SPLIT STYLE is an easy way for the very young one to eat soup. Make up soup with milk and heat thoroughly. Pour the nutritious broth into a cup for drinking; spoon the colorful solids onto a plate for eating.

BIRTHDAY SOUPS: Gay bowls of cream soup take on a party air when topped with a glowing birthday candle (set on a floating round of toast or a cracker). First top the cracker with a small ball of cream cheese or peanut butter. Poke the end of the candle into it and carefully slip the cracker onto the top of the soup. Then light up the candle.

SWIRLY SOUPS: Exciting to do and nourishing too. Let the youngsters swirl or write on the soup surface this way. Prepare soup as usual and pour into bowls. Slowly pour light cream, milk, reconstituted dry milk, or evaporated milk from a pitcher, back and forth across the soup. Stir with a soup spoon to make initials, animals, faces, or pretty marbled effects.

SNIPPETS: Good eating with soup are snippets of cheese. These are simply animals, numbers, stars, or other shapes that youngsters cut with cookie cutters from slices of process cheese. These float atop soup.

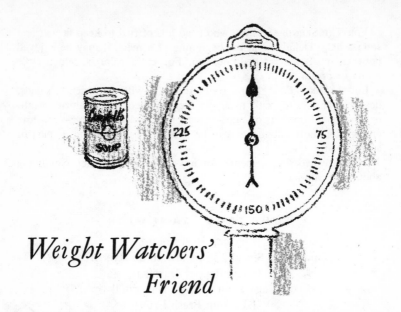

Weight Watchers' Friend

Calorie-conscious folks (those wanting to lose or gain weight) can survey the following soup groupings for calorie count.

Calories listed are per 10 ounce portions of prepared soup (based on the first directions listed on the label).

35 to 70 CALORIES: Beef broth, chicken broth, chicken gumbo, consommé.

70 to 100 CALORIES: Cream of asparagus, beef, beef noodle, chicken noodle, chicken noodle-O's, chicken with rice, chicken & stars, chicken vegetable, clam chowder (Manhattan Style), curly noodle with chicken, golden vegetable noodle-O's, golden mushroom, onion, Scotch broth, turkey noodle, turkey vegetable, vegetable, vegetable beef, old fashioned vegetable, vegetarian vegetable.

100 to 140 CALORIES: Black bean, cream of celery, cream of chicken, chicken 'n dumplings, minestrone, noodles & ground beef, pepper pot, cream of potato, stockpot, tomato, old fashioned tomato rice.

140 to 210 CALORIES: Bean with bacon, Cheddar cheese, chili beef, New England clam chowder, green pea, hot dog bean, cream of mushroom, cream of shrimp, oyster stew, split pea with ham, tomato-beef noodle-O's, tomato bisque.

Calories listed are per ½ can portion of chunky soup.

140 to 160 CALORIES: Chunky chicken with rice, chunky clam chowder (Manhattan Style), chunky turkey, chunky vegetable.

200 to 220 CALORIES: Chunky beef, chunky chicken, chunky sirloin burger, chunky split pea with ham.

145

FOR THE SLENDER: Those who need lots of fuel to keep fit will find soup a help. Delightful at the beginning of a meal, it may be enjoyed between meals and at bedtime, too. For extra calories, add a little butter or cream.

LOW-CALORIE TIPS: Many soups team up with sandwiches, salads, desserts, and skim milk to make well-balanced, low-calorie meals. In ½ cup portions, two soups—beef broth and consommé—are low enough in calories that they can be used without counting as part of a meal plan.

Here are two simple menus for low-calorie meals, each containing about 400 calories.

SOUP AND SANDWICH

¾ cup Beef Soup
Open-Face Sliced Egg Sandwich on Rye Bread
Green Pepper Garnish
1 Glass Skim Milk or Buttermilk
1 Portion Fresh Fruit

SOUP AND SALAD

¾ cup Cream of Celery Soup,
Prepared with Milk, 2 Saltines
Cold plate—2 ounces Sliced Lean Meat,
Chicken, or Turkey
Sliced Tomato and Dill Pickle Garnish
½ cup Orange and Grapefruit Compote

Low-calorie soups can be extra-flavorful, as in these recipes:

BEEF BROTH CHABLIS

1 can (10½ ounces) condensed beef broth
1 soup can water
2 tablespoons Chablis or other dry white wine

Combine all ingredients. Place in refrigerator for at least 4 hours. Serve in chilled cups or glasses. Makes about 2½ cups; 94 calories.

ENERGY BOOSTER

1 can (10¾ ounces) condensed
  tomato soup
1 soup can water
1 bay leaf
¼ teaspoon celery salt

In saucepan, combine all ingredients. Heat; simmer a few minutes to blend flavors. Remove bay leaf. Makes about 2½ cups; 220 calories.

CRESS BROTH

1 can (10½ ounces) condensed
  beef broth
1 soup can water
2 tablespoons minced watercress
Lemon wedges

Combine beef broth, water, and watercress Place in refrigerator for at least 4 hours. Serve in chilled mugs or bowls; garnish with lemon wedges. Makes about 2½ cups; 70 calories.

SPINACH TOMATO SOUP

1 cup chopped fresh spinach
1 tablespoon butter or margarine
1 can (10¾ ounces) condensed
  tomato soup
1 soup can water
¼ teaspoon ground nutmeg

In saucepan, cook spinach in butter 5 minutes. Blend in soup, water, and nutmeg. Heat; stir occasionally. Makes about 2½ cups; 331 calories.

CHICKEN VEGETABLE V-8

1 can (10½ ounces) condensed
  chicken vegetable soup
½ soup can V-8 juice
½ soup can water

In saucepan, combine soup, V-8 juice, and water. Heat; stir occasionally. Makes about 2½ cups; 215 calories.

BROTH PICK-UP

1 can (10½ ounces) condensed
  beef broth
1 can (10¾ ounces) condensed
  tomato soup
1 soup can water
½ teaspoon lemon juice
⅛ teaspoon sweet basil

In saucepan, combine all ingredients. Simmer a few minutes. Stir occasionally. Makes about 3½ cups; 290 calories.

Appetizer Soups

"Soup puts the heart at ease, calms down the violence of hunger, eliminates the tensions of the day, and awakens and refines the appetite."—Escoffier

Soup, hot or chilled, sets the mood for the meal to come. Soup can breathe of spring, or bring warmth to a cold winter's evening. Cool jellied consommé revives summer appetites, and robust soups add substance to an autumn meal. Bright soup can give the color contrast needed for a pale table setting. Clear broth is the gourmet's choice to set off elegant dinners. A tureen of soup makes a popular addition to a buffet, and the most welcome centerpiece of all, when the family gathers at the table. Happy is the family that can answer yes to

"Do daily soups
Your dinners introduce?"—John Gay

TOMATO MINESTRONE

1 can (10½ ounces) condensed
   minestrone soup
½ soup can water
½ soup can tomato juice

In saucepan, combine all ingredients. Heat. Makes about 2½ cups.

NUTMEG MUG

1 can (11¼ ounces) condensed
   green pea soup
1 soup can water or milk
⅛ to ¼ teaspoon ground nutmeg
Orange slices, cut in quarters

In saucepan, combine soup, water or milk, and nutmeg. Heat; stir occasionally. Serve in mugs or cups; garnish with orange slices. Makes about 2½ cups.

WHITE PUFF PEA SOUP

1 can (11¼ ounces) condensed
   green pea soup
1 soup can water
Dash ground cloves
1 teaspoon grated orange rind
⅓ cup heavy cream, whipped

In saucepan, combine soup, water, and cloves. Heat; stir occasionally. Fold orange rind into whipped cream. Top each serving with whipped cream. Makes about 2½ cups.

SOUP ITALIANO

1 can (11¼ ounces) condensed
   green pea soup
1 can (10¾ ounces) condensed
   tomato soup
1½ soup cans water
¼ cup Burgundy or other dry
   red wine
⅛ teaspoon Italian seasoning,
   crushed

In saucepan, blend soups; gradually stir in remaining ingredients. Simmer a few minutes to blend flavors; stir occasionally. Garnish with croutons. Makes about 4½ cups.

CREOLE SOUP

2 slices bacon
2 tablespoons chopped onion
1 can (11 ounces) condensed
   tomato rice soup
1 soup can water
½ cup cooked cut green beans

In saucepan, cook bacon until crisp; remove and crumble. Add onion; cook until tender. Add soup, water, and green beans. Heat; stir. Sprinkle with bacon. Makes about 3 cups.

CHILLED MINTED PEA SOUP

1 can (11¼ ounces) condensed
  green pea soup
1 soup can milk
¼ cup light cream
½ teaspoon dried mint flakes,
  crushed

Blend all ingredients. Chill at least
4 hours. Makes about 2½ cups.

ROSY TURKEY NOODLE SOUP

1 can (10¾ ounces) condensed
  turkey noodle soup
½ soup can water
½ soup can V-8 juice

In saucepan, combine all ingredients. Heat. Makes about 2½ cups.

SAFARI SIPPER

1 can (11 ounces) condensed
  Cheddar cheese soup
1 can (10¾ ounces) condensed
  tomato soup
1 soup can milk
1 soup can water

In saucepan, stir cheese soup until
smooth; gradually blend in tomato
soup, milk, and water. Heat; stir
occasionally. Makes about 5 cups.

CABARET CUP

1 can (10½ ounces) condensed
  beef broth
1 soup can water
2 tablespoons wine (sauterne,
  sherry, rosé, or Burgundy)
Orange or lemon slices, clove
  studded

In saucepan, combine beef broth
and water; add wine. Heat a few
minutes to blend flavors. Float
clove-studded orange or lemon
slices in broth. Makes about 2½
cups.

CONSOMMÉ JULIENNE

1 cup vegetables cut in thin strips
  (carrot, onion, green pepper,
  leek, parsnip)
1 tablespoon butter or margarine
2 cans (10½ ounces each)
  condensed consommé
2 soup cans water

In saucepan, cook vegetables in
butter until tender but still firm.
Add consommé and water. Heat;
stir. Makes about 6 cups.

CHILLY PICADILLY

1 can (10¾ ounces) condensed
  cream of mushroom soup
1 soup can milk
1 teaspoon minced chives or
  chopped fresh dill
Sour cream, if desired

Blend soup, milk, and seasoning. Chill at least 4 hours. Serve in chilled bowls. Garnish with dollop of sour cream. Makes about 2½ cups.

IRISH TUREEN

1 can (10¾ ounces) condensed
  cream of potato soup
1 soup can milk
½ cup cooked chopped broccoli

In saucepan, combine all ingredients. Heat; stir occasionally. Makes about 3 cups.

CREAMY POTATO POTAGE

½ cup finely chopped cucumber
2 tablespoons chopped green onion
2 tablespoons butter or margarine
1 can (10¾ ounces) condensed
  cream of potato soup
½ soup can milk
½ soup can water
⅓ cup sour cream
⅛ teaspoon paprika

In saucepan, cook cucumber and green onion in butter until tender. Add remaining ingredients. Heat; stir occasionally. To serve as cold soup, prepare as above. Chill 4 hours. Thin to desired consistency with milk. Makes about 3½ cups.

QUICK RHODE ISLAND CHOWDER

2 tablespoons chopped onion
⅛ teaspoon thyme leaves, crushed
2 tablespoons butter or margarine
1 can (10¾ ounces) condensed
  New England clam chowder
1 soup can milk
½ cup cooked peas

In saucepan, cook onion with thyme in butter until tender. Add soup, milk, and peas. Heat; stir occasionally. Makes about 2½ cups.

PARSLIED SHRIMP POTAGE

1 can (10¾ ounces) condensed
  cream of celery soup
1 soup can water
1 cup diced cooked shrimp
2 tablespoons chopped parsley
1 small clove garlic, minced

In saucepan, combine all ingredients. Heat; stir occasionally. Makes about 3½ cups.

SPRIG O' SPRING SOUP

1 can (10¾ ounces) condensed
   cream of asparagus soup
1 soup can milk
¼ bunch watercress (about ¼ cup)
⅛ teaspoon basil
Dash pepper

Blend all ingredients 2 minutes in electric blender, or chop watercress very fine and combine with other ingredients in saucepan. Heat; stir occasionally. Garnish with sprigs of watercress. Makes about 2½ cups.

HOT BUTTERED SOUP

1 can (10¾ ounces) condensed
   tomato soup
1 soup can water or milk
Butter

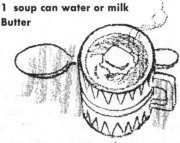

In saucepan, combine soup and water. Heat; stir occasionally. Pour into cups or mugs; garnish each with a pat of butter. Makes about 2½ cups. Try a butter pat atop cream of asparagus, celery, chicken, mushroom, and green pea soups, too, for extra cold or extra hungry soupsters.

BEEF BROTH WITH HORSERADISH

1 can (10½ ounces) condensed
   beef broth
1 cup water
½ teaspoon prepared horseradish
⅛ teaspoon dried dill leaves
Sour cream
Cucumber strips

In saucepan, combine soup, water, horseradish, and dill. Simmer a few minutes. Pour into cups or mugs and top each serving with dab of sour cream. Use cucumber strips as crisp stirrers. Makes about 2 cups.

TRIPLE PLAY WARMER

1 can (11¼ ounces) condensed
   green pea soup
1 can (10¾ ounces) condensed
   tomato soup
1 can (10½ ounces) condensed
   beef broth
2 soup cans milk
⅓ cup sherry

In saucepan, stir green pea and tomato soups until smooth. Gradually blend in remaining ingredients. Heat; stir occasionally. Makes about 6½ cups.

TOMATO-VEGETABLE

1 can (10¾ ounces) condensed
tomato soup
1 can (10½ ounces) condensed
vegetarian vegetable soup
1½ soup cans water

In saucepan, combine soups and
water. Heat; stir often. Makes about
4½ cups.

ROUNDUP CUP

1 can (10½ ounces) condensed
beef broth
1 can (12 fl. oz.) V-8 juice
1 teaspoon lemon juice
⅛ teaspoon sweet basil, crushed

In saucepan, combine beef broth,
V-8, lemon juice, and basil. Simmer
1 or 2 minutes. Makes about 2½
cups.

HAM 'N CHICKEN CHOWDER

½ cup cooked ham, cut in strips
1 tablespoon butter or margarine
1 can (10¾ ounces) condensed
cream of chicken soup
1 soup can water
½ cup cooked mixed vegetables

In saucepan, cook ham in butter
until lightly browned. Add remaining ingredients. Heat; stir often.
Makes about 3½ cups.

CHILLED TOMATO BOWL

1 can (10½ ounces) condensed
consommé
1 can (10¾ ounces) condensed
tomato soup
1 soup can water
½ cup chopped cucumber
1 teaspoon dried chives
Generous dash hot pepper sauce
Sour cream

Blend soups and water; add cucumber, chives, and hot pepper sauce.
Chill 4 hours or more. Serve in
chilled bowls; garnish with sour
cream. Makes about 4 cups.

HOPSCOTCH SOUP

1 can (10¾ ounces) condensed
beef noodle soup
1 can (10½ ounces) condensed
vegetable soup
1½ soup cans water

In saucepan, combine soups and
water. Heat; stir often. Makes
about 4½ cups.

153

CREAMY CHEESE BOWL

1 can (10¾ ounces) condensed
  cream of chicken soup
1 soup can water
½ cup shredded mild process cheese
2 tablespoons sauterne or other
  white wine
Generous dash garlic powder

In saucepan, combine all ingredients. Heat until cheese melts; stir often. Makes about 3 cups.

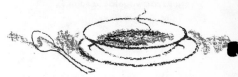

CHICKEN SOUP AMANDINE

1 can (10¾ ounces) condensed
  cream of chicken soup
1 soup can milk
¼ teaspoon grated onion
2 tablespoons chopped toasted
  almonds

In saucepan, combine soup, milk, and onion. Heat. Garnish with almonds. Makes about 2½ cups.

CURRIED CHICKEN SOUP

2 tablespoons chopped onion
1 tablespoon diced celery
1 to 2 teaspoons curry powder
1 tablespoon butter or margarine
1 can (10¾ ounces) condensed
  cream of chicken soup
½ soup can milk
½ soup can water
Toasted almonds or coconut

In saucepan, cook onion and celery with curry powder in butter until tender. Blend in soup, milk, and water. Heat; stir occasionally. Garnish with almonds or coconut. Makes about 2½ cups.

TOMATO GUMBO

1 can (10¾ ounces) condensed
  chicken gumbo soup
½ soup can tomato juice
½ soup can water

In saucepan, combine all ingredients. Heat; stir. Makes about 2½ cups.

HERBED CONSOMMÉ

1 can (10½ ounces) condensed
  consommé
1 soup can water
Dash dill seed, tarragon, or basil

In saucepan, combine all ingredients. Heat; simmer a few minutes. Garnish, if desired, with toast squares. Makes about 2½ cups.

CURRIED COCONUT SHRIMP SOUP

2 teaspoons butter or margarine
¼ teaspoon curry powder
¼ cup flaked coconut
1 can (10¾ ounces) condensed
   cream of chicken soup
1 soup can milk
1 cup diced cooked shrimp

In small saucepan, melt butter; stir in curry powder; add coconut. Cook, stirring until lightly toasted. Meanwhile, in another saucepan, combine remaining ingredients. Heat; stir occasionally. Garnish with curried coconut. Makes about 3½ cups.

CLAM DIGGERS' CUP

1 can (10¾ ounces) condensed
   tomato soup
1 cup clam juice
¼ cup water

In saucepan, combine all ingredients. Heat; stir occasionally. Makes about 5½ cups.

ZIPPY TOMATO SOUP

1 can (10¾ ounces) condensed
   tomato soup
1 soup can water
½ teaspoon prepared horseradish
¼ teaspoon Worcestershire
Dash dry mustard

In saucepan, combine all ingredients. Simmer 5 minutes; stir often. Makes about 2½ cups.

BUTTERMILK BREW

1 can (10¾ ounces) condensed
   tomato soup
1 cup water
⅓ cup buttermilk
¼ cup chopped cucumber
⅛ teaspoon dried dill leaves,
   crushed

In saucepan, combine all ingredients. Heat; stir occasionally. Chill 6 hours or more. Makes about 2½ cups.

EAST INDIA TOMATO SOUP

2 tablespoons thinly sliced green
   onion
1 tablespoon butter or margarine
1 can (10¾ ounces) condensed
   tomato soup
1 soup can water
¼ teaspoon curry powder

In saucepan, cook green onion in butter until lightly browned. Add soup, water, and curry powder. Heat; stir. Serve hot or chill at least 4 hours and serve. Makes about 2½ cups.

HEARTY BEEF WARM-UP

1 cup sliced fresh mushrooms
  (about ¼ pound)
1 small green pepper, cut in strips
1 tablespoon butter or margarine
1 can (10¾ ounces) condensed
  beef noodle soup
1 can (11 ounces) condensed
  beef soup
2 soup cans water

In saucepan, brown mushrooms and cook green pepper in butter until tender. Add soups and water. Heat; stir occasionally. Makes about 5½ cups.

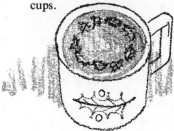

CHRISTMAS NOODLE CUP

1 can (10¾ ounces) condensed
  beef noodle soup
1 soup can water
1 teaspoon finely chopped parsley
1 teaspoon chopped pimiento

In saucepan, combine all ingredients. Heat; stir often. Garnish with wreath of chopped parsley or red bell cut from pimiento. Makes about 2½ cups.

BLACK BEAN FLOAT

2 cans (11 ounces each) condensed
  black bean soup
2 soup cans water
1 teaspoon instant minced onion
1 teaspoon lemon juice
½ cup sour cream
1 tablespoon chopped parsley
1 tablespoon chopped radish

In saucepan, combine soup, water, onion, and lemon juice. Heat; stir occasionally. Meanwhile, combine sour cream, parsley, and radish; serve as a garnish on soup. Makes about 5½ cups.

SPICED SIPPER

1 can (10¾ ounces) condensed
  cream of celery soup
1 can (10¾ ounces) condensed
  tomato soup
1 cup water
1 cup milk
Dash ground cloves
Chopped toasted almonds, if desired

In saucepan, blend soups, water, milk, and cloves. Heat; stir occasionally; sprinkle each serving with chopped almonds. Makes about 4½ cups.

V-8 VEGETABLE POTAGE

1 can (10½ ounces) condensed
  vegetable soup
½ soup can V-8 juice
½ soup can water

In saucepan, combine all ingredients. Heat. Garnish with popcorn, if desired. Makes about 2½ cups.

CHILLED GARDEN BOWL

1 can (10¾ ounces) condensed
  cream of celery soup
1 soup can water
½ cup chopped tomato
2 tablespoons chopped green onion
2 tablespoons chopped green
  pepper
¼ cup sour cream

Combine all ingredients; chill. Serve in chilled bowls. Makes about 3 cups.

COUNTRY FAIR SOUP

¼ cup diced cooked ham
1 tablespoon butter or margarine
Dash ground marjoram, if desired
1 can (10½ ounces) condensed
  turkey vegetable soup
1 soup can water

In saucepan, brown ham in butter with marjoram. Add soup and water. Heat. Makes about 2½ cups.

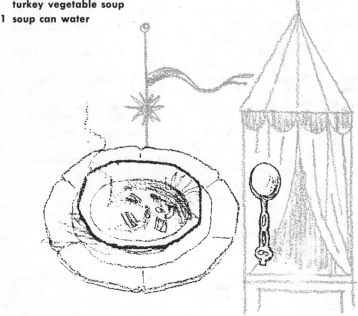

SOUP MATES...MIX-MATCH SOUPS

One soup	+Second soup+Liquid		=Soup Mate
Cream of Asparagus	Cream of Chicken	1½ cans milk or water	Heat, stir. Garnish with shreds of orange peel.
Cream of Asparagus	Scotch Broth	1½ cans water	Heat, stir. New lunch flavor.
Bean with Bacon or Hot Dog Bean	Minestrone	1½ cans water	Heat, stir. Ladle from bean pot.
Beef	Pepper Pot	2 cans water	Heat, stir. Dot with popcorn.
Beef	Tomato	2 cans water	Heat, stir. Add 1 teaspoon Sherry, if desired. Top with chopped parsley or chives.
Beef	Tomato Rice	1½ cans water	Heat, stir. Winter picnic warmup.
Beef Broth	Beef Noodle	1½ cans water	Heat, stir. Topping of herb-seasoned stuffing.
Beef Broth	Tomato	1½ cans water	Heat, stir. Float toast squares on top.
Beef Noodle	Minestrone	2 cans water	Heat, stir. Pack in lunchbox in vacuum.
Beef Noodle	Tomato	1½ cans water	Heat, stir. Ladle from bright casserole.
Beef Noodle	Vegetable Beef	1½ cans water	Heat, stir. Sprinkle with grated cheese.
Black Bean	Consommé	1½ cans water	Heat, stir. Garnish with lemon slices.
Cheddar Cheese	**Tomato Bisque**	1 can each milk and water	Heat, stir. Elegant in chowder mugs.
Chicken & Stars	Chicken Noodle	2 cans water	Heat. This makes "Stars and Stripes" for patriotic party themes.
Chicken 'n Dumplings	Vegetable	1½ to 2 cans water	Heat, stir. Perfect party appetizer.
Chicken Noodle	Vegetarian Vegetable	1½ cans water	Heat, stir. Accompaniment to cold sliced beef.
Chicken with Rice	Tomato	1½ cans water	Heat, stir. China soup cups on silver tray.
Chicken Vegetable	Golden Vegetable Noodle-O's	1½ to 2 cans water	Heat, stir. Cheese cubes afloat.
Chili Beef	Vegetable Beef	2 cans water	Heat, stir. Pass "Goldfish" crackers.
Cream of Celery	Chicken Vegetable	1 can water and 1 can milk	Heat, stir. Stirrers: cucumber spears.

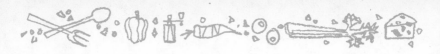

SOUP MATES...MIX-MATCH SOUPS

One soup	+Second soup	+Liquid	
Cream of Chicken	Chicken Noodle-O's	2 cans water or milk	Heat, stir. Add dash of curry or coconut, if desired.
Cream of Chicken	Chicken with Rice	1½ to 2 cans water or milk	Heat, stir. Break in breakfast routine; top with crisp cereal.
Cream of Mushroom	Cream of Asparagus	2 cans milk, or 1 can milk and 1 can water	Stir mushroom soup to smooth. Blend in asparagus soup and liquid. Heat; stir. Top with watercress.
Cream of Mushroom	Chicken with Rice	1½ cans milk or water	Stir mushroom soup to smooth. Blend in other soup and liquid. Heat, stir. Form family "soup line."
Cream of Mushroom	Consommé	1½ cans water	Stir mushroom soup to smooth. Blend in other soup and liquid. Heat, stir. Top with toasted almonds.
Tomato-Beef Noodle-O's	Vegetable	2 cans water	Heat, stir. Serve with garnish of sieved egg yolk.
Consommé	Scotch Broth	1½ cans water	Heat, stir. Cheese crackers to munch.
Consommé	Tomato Bisque	1 can each milk and water	Mix and heat. Garnish with sour cream.
Green Pea	Scotch Broth	1½ cans water	Heat, stir. Serve with party rye slices.
Noodles & Ground Beef	Old Fashioned Vegetable	2 cans water	Heat this hearty combination to enjoy with egg salad sandwich.
Onion	Stockpot	1½ cans water	Good with French bread.
Pepper Pot	Vegetable Beef	2 cans water	Heat, stir. Savor at Saturday lunch.
Turkey Noodle	Vegetable	1½ cans water	Heat, stir. Keep warm in chafing dish or electric kettle.

Great Soups

A salute to the classics—those distinctive soups that have long been an important part of the world's outstanding cuisines. What makes them unique? Each unites the best of its country's lands, seas, and traditions. Each speaks the universal language of excellence.

In French port towns, it's bouillabaisse. In French farm country, it's green pea and onion. In Scotland, barley goes into the broth. In India, curry reigns supreme.

In Maryland, U.S.A., the crab makes a great bisque. In New England, clam is the chowder choice. Everywhere, U.S.A., the ruddy farm tomato becomes America's favorite soup.

The art of soup-making contributes a fascinating chapter to world history. Back in the twelfth century, soup-making was such a refined skill that sometimes five or six kinds were served at a single meal.

In 1765 an enterprizing Paris tradesman, Monsieur Boulanger, began selling bowls of soup which could be bought at any hour. He called them "restaurantes" or pickups. So popular were they that the custom spread, and eventually additional dishes were offered as well.

With canned soups handy, you can offer "restaurantes" at any hour, too. Here is a selection of all-time greats.

CLAM CHOWDER

Clam chowder, named for the French *chaudier* in which it was cooked in Brittany, is canned now in creamy New England style as well as rosy Manhattan variety with tomatoes and other vegetables . . . and never the partisans of each shall meet. Both appetites can be readily satisfied. Prepared chowders are quick to heat and serve, making, as an old recipe puts it, "a dish fit for the best of the nation."

MULLIGATAWNY SOUP

Mulligatawny means "Pepper water" in India, a curry-flavored soup.

2 cans (10¾ ounces each) condensed cream of chicken soup
1 can (10½ ounces) condensed chicken with rice soup
1 teaspoon curry powder
2 soup cans water

In saucepan, blend soups and curry; gradually stir in water. Heat; stir occasionally. Makes about 6½ cups.

QUICK MOCK BOUILLABAISSE

Streamlined version of the fish stew native to Marseilles.

1 small onion, sliced
1 small clove garlic, minced
¼ teaspoon thyme leaves, crushed
2 tablespoons olive oil
1 can (10¾ ounces) condensed tomato soup
1 soup can water
2 cups cut-up cooked seafood (crab, fish, lobster, or shrimp)
1 small bay leaf
1 teaspoon lemon juice
Generous dash hot pepper sauce
4 slices French bread, toasted

In saucepan, cook onion with garlic and thyme in olive oil until tender. Add soup, water, seafood, bay leaf, lemon juice, and hot pepper sauce. Heat; stir occasionally. To serve, ladle soup over bread in bowls. Makes about 4 cups.

POTAGE A LA CRECY

1 can (10¾ ounces) condensed chicken broth
3 cups sliced raw carrots (about 1 pound)
¼ cup chopped celery
2 tablespoons chopped onion
1 soup can light cream
½ soup can milk
¼ teaspoon nutmeg

In saucepan, combine broth, carrots, celery, and onion. Cover; cook 20 minutes or until carrots are very tender. Blend in electric blender until smooth. In saucepan, combine all ingredients. Heat; stir occasionally. Makes about 4½ cups.

CIOPPINO

Glorified fish soup, a specialty at California's Fisherman's Wharf.

½ cup chopped green pepper
½ cup chopped onion
¼ teaspoon basil leaves, crushed
2 medium cloves garlic, minced
2 tablespoons olive oil
2 cans (10¾ ounces each)
    condensed tomato soup
1 soup can water
2 tablespoons chopped parsley
1 medium bay leaf
⅛ teaspoon grated lemon rind
⅛ teaspoon salt
2 teaspoons lemon juice
⅛ teaspoon hot pepper sauce
1 pound fish fillets, cut in
    2-inch pieces
1 pound medium shrimp (about 30),
    cleaned and cut up
1 cup cooked crab meat, flaked

In large saucepan, cook green pepper and onion with basil and garlic in olive oil until tender. Stir in remaining ingredients except crab. Bring to boil; reduce heat. Simmer 10 minutes or until fish is done. Add crab. Heat; stir occasionally. Makes about 8 cups.

MARYLAND BISQUE

A Peninsula blend of flavors you can make quickly.

2 cans (10½ ounces each)
    condensed oyster stew
2 soup cans milk
2 cups diced cooked potatoes
2 tablespoons chopped parsley

In saucepan, combine all ingredients. Heat; stir occasionally. Makes about 5½ cups.

YANKEE CHOWDER

A rugged inland blend of what's handy for the big soup pot.

1 can (10¾ ounces) condensed
    cream of mushroom soup
3 soup cans water
1 can (10¾ ounces) condensed
    turkey noodle soup
1 can (10½ ounces) condensed
    vegetarian vegetable soup

Stir mushroom soup until smooth in large saucepan; gradually blend in water. Add remaining soups. Heat; stir occasionally. Makes about 7½ cups.

CHICKEN CHOWDER

Potatoes and chicken in a creamy blend, Massachusetts farm choice.

½ cup chopped celery
1 tablespoon butter or margarine
1 can (10¾ ounces) condensed
  potato soup
1 soup can milk
1 can (5 ounces) boned chicken or
  turkey, cut up
1 tablespoon chopped parsley

In saucepan, cook celery in butter until tender. Add remaining ingredients. Heat; stir occasionally. Makes about 3½ cups.

GUMBO

New Orleans soup with shrimp and ham.

½ cup diced cooked ham
¼ cup chopped celery
¼ cup chopped green pepper
¼ cup chopped onion
⅛ teaspoon thyme leaves, crushed
2 tablespoons butter or margarine
2 cans (10¾ ounces each)
  condensed chicken gumbo soup
1½ soup cans water
1 cup frozen cleaned raw shrimp

In saucepan, brown ham and cook celery, green pepper, and onion with thyme in butter until tender. Add remaining ingredients. Bring to boil; reduce heat. Simmer 5 minutes or until shrimp is done. Stir occasionally. Makes about 5½ cups.

GREEK LEMON SOUP

"Soup Avgolemono" to the Greeks, this has rare delicate tang.

1 can (10½ ounces) condensed
  chicken with rice soup
1 soup can water
1 egg
2 teaspoons lemon juice
Nutmeg
Butter

In saucepan, blend soup and water; heat. Meanwhile, beat egg and lemon juice together in small bowl until well blended. Add a little hot soup to egg mixture; stir constantly. Remove remaining soup from heat; slowly stir in egg mixture (this method prevents curdling). Serve immediately. Garnish with nutmeg or butter, if desired. Makes about 2½ cups.

MARDI GRAS

Okra, crab, and rice in a flavorful base, gay as the Mardi Gras!

1 can (10¾ ounces) condensed
  chicken gumbo soup
1 can (10¾ ounces) condensed
  tomato soup
2 soup cans water
½ cup quick-cooking rice, uncooked
1 can (7 ounces) crab meat,
  drained and flaked

In saucepan, combine all ingredients except crab. Bring to boil; cover. Reduce heat; simmer 5 minutes or until rice is done. Stir occasionally. Add crab; heat. Makes about 5½ cups.

WILLIAMSBURG PUMPKIN SOUP

Pumpkin purée blends with creamy chicken, a Colonial discovery.

¼ cup finely chopped onion
4 tablespoons butter or margarine
1 can (10¾ ounces) condensed
  cream of chicken or
  mushroom soup
1 cup canned or mashed cooked
  pumpkin
½ teaspoon ground nutmeg
½ teaspoon sugar
¼ teaspoon salt
Dash pepper
1 soup can water

In saucepan, cook onion in butter until tender. Stir in soup, pumpkin, and seasonings; gradually add water. Heat; stir occasionally. Garnish with parsley. Makes about 2½ cups.

POLISH CABBAGE SOUP

A Balkan stew-soup to make a supper.

½ pound lean boneless pork, diced
1 tablespoon shortening
1 can (10½ ounces) condensed
  beef broth
1 can (10¾ ounces) condensed
  tomato soup
2 soup cans water
4 cups cabbage cut in long thin
  shreds (about 1 pound)
½ cup chopped onion
1 teaspoon salt
½ teaspoon paprika
1 small bay leaf
Generous dash pepper
Sour cream

In saucepan, brown pork in shortening; pour off fat. Add remaining ingredients except sour cream. Cover; cook over low heat 30 minutes. Stir occasionally. Garnish with sour cream. Makes about 7 cups.

COCK-A-LEEKIE

*Scottish wives simmer chicken with leeks and vegetables, serve soup one day,
chicken the next. The prunes—a tasty tradition.*

1½ cups thinly sliced leeks or
green onions
2 tablespoons butter or margarine
2 cans (10½ ounces each)
condensed chicken vegetable soup
2 soup cans water
¼ cup chopped canned pitted
prunes
Dash pepper

In saucepan, cook leeks in butter
until tender. Add remaining ingredients. Heat; stir occasionally.
Makes about 6 cups.

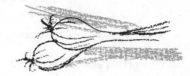

GOULASH SOUP

1 cup cubed cooked beef
¼ cup chopped green pepper
½ teaspoon paprika
2 tablespoons butter or margarine
1 can (10¾ ounces) condensed
tomato soup
1 soup can water
½ teaspoon caraway seed

In saucepan, brown beef and cook
green pepper and paprika in butter
until green pepper is tender. Add
remaining ingredients. Heat; stir
occasionally. Makes about 3 cups.

HEARTLAND CHOWDER

⅓ cup shredded cabbage
⅓ cup grated carrot
¼ cup chopped onion
2 tablespoons butter or margarine
1 can (11¼ ounces) condensed
green pea soup
1 soup can water

In saucepan, cook cabbage, carrot,
and onion in butter until tender.
Add soup and water. Heat; stir
occasionally. Makes about 3 cups.

POTAGE ST. GERMAIN

This tangy pea soup with chicken is justly famed in France.

1 can (10¾ ounces) condensed
cream of chicken soup
1 can (11¼ ounces) condensed
green pea soup
2 cups milk
½ cup heavy cream
½ cup cooked sliced carrot

In saucepan, stir soups, milk, and
cream until smooth. Add carrot.
Heat; stir often. Makes about 5
cups.

PURÉE MONGOLE

A purée is sieved—but you need no strainer for this combination.

1 can (11¼ ounces) condensed green pea soup
1 can (10¾ ounces) condensed tomato soup
1 cup milk
1 cup water

In saucepan, blend soups, milk, and water. Heat; stir. Add a dash of curry powder, if desired. Makes about 4½ cups.

PERK-ME-UP-CUP

½ cup sliced celery
¼ cup chopped green pepper
1 tablespoon butter or margarine
1 can (10½ ounces) condensed beef broth
1 soup can water
2 tablespoons diced pimiento
⅛ teaspoon hot pepper sauce

In saucepan, cook celery and green pepper in butter until tender. Add remaining ingredients. Heat; stir occasionally. Makes about 3½ cups.

MEXICAN FOAM SOUP

¼ cup chopped onion
2 tablespoons chopped green pepper
1 tablespoon butter or margarine
1 can (10¾ ounces) condensed tomato soup
1 soup can milk
Generous dash cayenne pepper
1 egg, separated

In saucepan, cook onion and green pepper in butter until tender. Stir in soup, milk, and pepper. Slightly beat egg yolk. Stir a little hot soup mixture into yolk; gradually add to soup. Heat. Beat egg white until very soft peaks form. Add ½ cup soup mixture; beat lightly. Pour on top of soup. Makes about 2½ cups.

Williamsburg Pumpkin Soup   Page 164

BORSCH

There is rare color and flavor in the bright Russian peasant soup.

1 can (16 ounces) whole beets
2 cans (10½ ounces each)
    condensed consommé
1 tablespoon lemon juice
Water
Sour cream

Drain beets, saving juice. Chop beets. In saucepan, combine consommé, beets, and lemon juice. Add enough water to beet juice to measure 1 soup can; add to consommé mixture. Heat; stir occasionally. Garnish with sour cream. Makes about 5 cups.
Chilled Version: Prepare as above. Chill 6 hours or more. Serve in chilled bowls.

FRENCH ONION SOUP

1 can (10½ ounces) condensed
    onion soup
1 soup can water
2 or 3 slices French or Italian bread
    (about ½" thick)
Butter
Grated Parmesan cheese

In saucepan, combine soup and water. Heat; let simmer a few minutes. Meanwhile, arrange bread on cookie sheet; spread with butter and sprinkle with Parmesan cheese. Broil until lightly browned. Pour soup into bowls; top each with a cheese crouton. Makes about 2½ cups.

GREEN PEA FRANÇAIS

In 17th Century France, peas were the food of kings . . . kingly still.

1 can (about 2 ounces) mushroom
    stems and pieces, undrained
1 cup grated carrots
¼ teaspoon dried mint leaves,
    crushed
2 tablespoons butter or margarine
2 cans (11¼ ounces each)
    condensed green pea soup
2 soup cans water

Drain mushrooms, saving liquid. In saucepan, brown mushrooms and cook carrots with mint in butter until tender. Stir in soup; gradually blend in water and mushroom liquid. Heat; stir occasionally. Makes about 6 cups.

Old Fashioned Gingerbread Cake   Page 85

169

SENEGALESE SOUP

Curry and chicken have an affinity in the soup bowl, too.

1 can (10¾ ounces) condensed cream of chicken soup
⅛ teaspoon curry powder
1 soup can milk

Stir soup; blend in curry powder. Add milk gradually. Place in refrigerator for at least 4 hours. Serve in chilled bowls. Makes about 2½ cups.

VATAPA

Unusual South American blend of broth, shellfish, nuts.

1 can (10½ ounces) condensed beef broth
2 cans (10¾ ounces each) condensed Manhattan style clam chowder
2 soup cans water
½ cup chopped salted peanuts
¼ cup shredded coconut
1 bay leaf
Dash hot pepper sauce
1 pound fresh shrimp, shelled, deveined, and cut up

In large saucepan, combine all ingredients except shrimp. Cover; bring to boil. Add shrimp; cook over low heat 5 minutes or until tender. Stir occasionally. Remove bay leaf before serving. Makes about 8 cups.

HAMMED-UP CHOWDER

2 slices bacon
½ cup diced ham
⅓ cup green pepper strips
2 cans (10¾ ounces each) condensed cream of shrimp soup
1 soup can milk
1 soup can water
½ cup cooked rice

In saucepan, cook bacon until crisp; remove and crumble. Brown ham and cook green pepper in drippings until tender. Add remaining ingredients. Heat; stir occasionally. Garnish with bacon. Makes about 6 cups.

TURKEY VEGETABLE CUP

1 can (about 2 ounces) mushroom stems and pieces, drained
Generous dash crushed thyme leaves
1 tablespoon butter or margarine
1 can (10½ ounces) condensed turkey vegetable soup
1 soup can water

In saucepan, brown mushrooms with thyme in butter. Stir in soup and water. Heat; stir occasionally. Makes about 2½ cups.

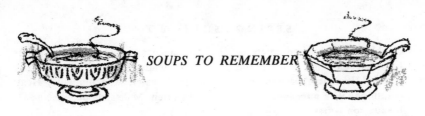

You, too, can indulge in a bit of nostalgia simply by rustling up tantalizing soups reminiscent of iron kettles and wood-burning stoves. With condensed soups, it's easy—as the following recipes demonstrate. Try some on for taste. You won't soon forget them.

MAINE FISH SOUP

½ cup chopped onion
1 tablespoon butter or margarine
1 can (10¾ ounces) condensed cream of celery soup
1 can (10¾ ounces) condensed Manhattan style clam chowder
1½ soup cans water
1 cup flaked cooked white fish or tuna (7-ounce can, drained and flaked) or shrimp (6-ounce can, drained)
1 tablespoon chopped parsley

In saucepan, cook onion in butter until tender. Blend in remaining ingredients. Simmer a few minutes; stir often. Makes about 5½ cups.

BEANSTRONI

1 cup diced cooked ham
2 tablespoons chopped onion
1 tablespoon butter or margarine
1 can (11½ ounces) bean with bacon soup
2 soup cans water
1 can (10½ ounces) condensed minestrone soup

In saucepan, brown ham and onion in butter. Stir in bean with bacon soup; blend in water. Add minestrone soup. Heat; stir often. Makes about 5 cups.

MEATBALL SOUP

½ pound ground beef, seasoned
1 can (11½ ounces) condensed bean with bacon, celery, mushroom, green pea, minestrone, onion, tomato, or vegetable soup
1 soup can water

Shape meat into 20 small meatballs; brown slowly in saucepan. (Use a little shortening if necessary.) Pour off any excess drippings. Stir in soup and water; simmer a few minutes. Makes about 3½ cups.

SPRING SOUP BOWL

2 tablespoons chopped onion
1 tablespoon butter or margarine
1 can (11½ ounces) condensed
    split pea with ham soup
1 soup can water
2 tablespoons chopped pimiento

In saucepan, cook onion in butter until tender. Add soup; gradually stir in water. Add pimiento. Heat; stir often. Makes about 2½ cups.

COUNTRY FAVORITE

2 slices bacon
2 tablespoons chopped onion
Dash crushed thyme leaves
1 can (10¾ ounces) condensed
    beef noodle soup
1 soup can water
½ cup cooked cut green beans

In saucepan, cook bacon until crisp; remove and crumble. Pour off all but 1 tablespoon drippings. Cook onion with thyme in drippings until tender. Add soup, water, and beans. Heat; stir occasionally. Garnish with bacon. Makes about 3 cups.

VEGETABLE FRANKFURTER SOUP

1 frankfurter, thinly sliced
2 tablespoons chopped onion
1 tablespoon butter or margarine
1 can (10½ ounces) condensed
    old fashioned vegetable soup
1 soup can water

In saucepan, brown frankfurter and cook onion in butter until tender. Stir in soup and water. Heat; stir occasionally. Makes about 3 cups.

CANADIAN COUNTRY SOUP

½ cup chopped onion
1 tablespoon butter or margarine
1 can (11½ ounces) condensed
    bean with bacon soup
1 can (10¾ ounces) condensed
    cream of mushroom soup
1 can (10½ ounces) condensed
    vegetarian vegetable soup
2 soup cans water
4 slices (about 4 ounces) Canadian
    bacon, cut in strips
1 can (about 8 ounces) whole
    kernel corn, drained

In saucepan, cook onion in butter until tender. Blend in soups; gradually stir in water. Add bacon and corn. Heat; stir occasionally. Makes about 7½ cups.

SOUTHERN BEEF SOUP

¼ cup chopped onion
2 tablespoons butter or margarine
1 can (10¾ ounces) condensed
   cream of celery soup
1 can (10¾ ounces) condensed
   cream of mushroom soup
1 soup can water
½ soup can milk
1 jar (about 2 ounces) sliced dried
   beef, rinsed and chopped
1 cup cooked succotash
½ cup chopped canned tomatoes

In saucepan, cook onion in butter until tender. Blend in soups; gradually stir in water and milk. Add remaining ingredients. Heat; stir occasionally. Makes about 6½ cups.

CRAB BISQUE

¼ cup chopped onion
⅛ teaspoon leaf thyme
1 tablespoon butter or margarine
1 can (11 ounces) condensed
   Cheddar cheese soup
½ soup can milk
½ soup can water
1 cup flaked cooked crab meat
   (or 7-ounce can, drained)
¼ cup chopped cooked broccoli
Lemon wedges

In saucepan, cook onion and thyme in butter until onion is tender. Add remaining ingredients except lemon wedges. Heat; stir often. Serve with lemon wedges. Makes about 3½ cups.

FIRESIDE TUREEN

¼ cup chopped onion
1 tablespoon butter or margarine
1 can (10¾ ounces) condensed
   cream of celery soup
1 can (10¾ ounces) condensed
   turkey noodle soup
1 cup milk
1 cup water
1 can (about 8 ounces) cream style
   corn
Chopped parsley

In saucepan, cook onion in butter until tender. Blend in soups, milk, and water; add corn. Heat; stir occasionally. Garnish with parsley. Makes about 5½ cups.

CHICKEN MUSHROOM POTAGE

1 can (10¾ ounces) condensed
   cream of mushroom soup
1 can (10½ ounces) condensed
   chicken vegetable soup
1½ soup cans water
1 cup cooked chopped spinach
1 cup diced cooked ham

In saucepan, combine soups; gradually blend in water. Add remaining ingredients. Heat; stir occasionally. Makes about 5½ cups.

CHICKEN CANJA

½ cup diced cooked ham
1 tablespoon butter or margarine
1 can (10¾ ounces) condensed
   cream of chicken soup
1 can (10½ ounces) condensed
   chicken vegetable soup
2 soup cans water
1 tablespoon chopped parsley

In saucepan, lightly brown ham in butter. Blend in soups, water, and parsley. Heat; stir often. Makes about 5 cups.

SHRIMP-POTATO SOUP

2 cans (10¾ ounces each)
   condensed cream of potato soup
2 soup cans milk
1 cup diced cooked shrimp
½ cup cooked whole kernel corn
¼ cup chopped parsley
Generous dash hot pepper sauce

In saucepan, combine all ingredients. Heat; stir occasionally. Makes about 6 cups.

TUNA VEGETABLE BOWL

2 tablespoons chopped onion
Generous dash crushed thyme leaves
2 tablespoons butter or margarine
1 can (10¾ ounces) condensed
   cream of celery soup
1 can (10½ ounces) condensed
   vegetarian vegetable soup
2 soup cans water
1 can (about 7 ounces) tuna,
   drained and flaked
2 tablespoons chopped parsley

In saucepan, cook onion with thyme in butter until tender. Blend in soups and water; add tuna and parsley. Heat; stir occasionally. Makes about 6 cups.

Frosty Soups

Some like it cold! And for good reason. Chilled summer soups make enticing appetizers. What could be so inviting as creamy smooth vichyssoise set out in ice-lined bowls, or shimmering jellied consommé garnished with fresh vegetables? Frosty sippers guarantee cool refreshment at pick-up time, too.

Cold soups were made fashionable back in the seventeenth century by Louis XIV—for a very practical reason. Each of the king's dishes was tasted by several people before it came to him. The monarch grew tired of lukewarm soup, and requested tasty cold soups, instead.

EPICURE'S COCKTAIL

2 cans (10½ ounces each)
   condensed beef broth, chilled
1 soup can ice water
½ cup orange juice
2 to 4 tablespoons lemon juice
½ teaspoon aromatic bitters
½ teaspoon sugar
Orange slices

In container with lid, combine all ingredients except orange slices. Cover and shake well. Serve over ice cubes in chilled glasses. Garnish with orange slices. Makes about 4 cups.

CALIFORNIA COOLER

1 can (10¾ ounces) condensed
   cream of chicken soup
1 soup can milk
½ cup chopped celery
1 tablespoon chopped onion
1 ripe medium avocado, cut up

In saucepan, combine all ingredients except avocado. Heat; stir occasionally. Chill 6 hours or more. In blender, blend soup mixture and avocado until smooth. Thin to desired consistency with milk. Serve immediately. Makes about 3½ cups.

BLACK FROST

1 can (11 ounces) condensed
   black bean soup
1 can (10½ ounces) condensed
   consommé
1 soup can water
1 to 2 teaspoons sherry (optional)
Lemon slices

Stir black bean soup well; add consommé, water, and sherry. Heat; stir occasionally. Chill 6 hours or more. Serve in icy cold bowls. Garnish each serving with a lemon slice. Makes about 3½ cups.

CRAB BOWL

1 can (10¾ ounces) condensed
   cream of celery soup
1 soup can water
½ cup flaked cooked crab meat
1 tablespoon thinly sliced
   green onion
¼ teaspoon grated lemon rind
1 small tomato, diced
Lemon wedges

In saucepan, blend soup; gradually stir in water. Add crab, onion, and lemon rind. Heat; stir occasionally. Chill 6 hours or more. Stir in tomato. Serve in chilled bowls; garnish with lemon wedges. Makes about 3½ cups.

DUTCH POTAGE

1 cup shredded cabbage
¼ cup shredded carrot
¼ teaspoon caraway seed
1 tablespoon butter or margarine
1 can (10¾ ounces) condensed
   cream of potato soup
1 cup milk
½ cup sour cream

In saucepan, cook cabbage and carrot with caraway in butter until tender. Add remaining ingredients. Heat; stir occasionally. Chill 6 hours or more. Thin to desired consistency. Serve in chilled bowls. Makes about 3 cups.

CUCUMBER COOLER

1 can (10¾ ounces) condensed
   cream of celery soup
1 cup milk
1 small cucumber, diced
   (about 1 cup)
Dash hot pepper sauce
Dash salt and pepper
1 cup sour cream

Combine soup, milk, cucumber, hot pepper sauce, and seasonings in electric blender; blend for 2 minutes. Stir in sour cream. Chill 4 hours or more. Serve in chilled bowls. Makes about 3½ cups.

JELLIED CONSOMMÉ CALCUTTA

2 cans (10½ ounces each)
  condensed consommé
¼ cup diced green pepper
2 tablespoons chopped parsley
1 tablespoon finely chopped onion
¼ cup slivered almonds
½ teaspoon curry powder
1 tablespoon butter or margarine

Chill consommé until slightly thickened; stir occasionally. Fold in green pepper, parsley, and onion. Chill until jellied. In small skillet, brown almonds with curry in butter. Serve consommé in chilled bowls; top with almonds. Makes about 3 cups.

SHRIMP DELIGHT

2 cans (10½ ounces each)
  condensed consommé
2 tablespoons lemon juice
Dash hot pepper sauce
1 can (about 4 ounces) shrimp,
  drained
¼ cup chopped celery
2 tablespoons chopped
  green onions
Avocado slices

Combine consommé, lemon juice, and hot pepper sauce. Chill until slightly thickened; stir occasionally. Fold in shrimp, celery, and onion. Chill until jellied. Serve in chilled bowls. Garnish with avocado. Makes about 3 cups.

GAZPACHO

1 can (10¾ ounces) condensed
  tomato soup
1 cup water
1 tablespoon olive oil
2 tablespoons wine vinegar
1 large clove garlic, minced
1 cup finely chopped cucumber
½ cup finely chopped green pepper
¼ cup finely chopped onion

In bowl, combine soup, water, oil, vinegar, and garlic. Chill 4 hours. Serve in chilled bowls. Pass chilled vegetables for garnishes (also croutons if desired). Makes about 2 cups.

PARFAIT CONSOMMÉ

1 can (10½ ounces) condensed
  consommé
½ cup sour cream
2 tablespoons chopped chives

Place unopened can of consommé in refrigerator until jellied, about 4 hours. To serve, spoon a little consommé into each parfait glass; top with sour cream. Repeat layers; sprinkle chives on top. Makes about 1 cup.

SOUP-ON-THE-ROCKS

The easiest and most popular of frosted soups is yours to enjoy anywhere. Simply fill a broad glass with ice cubes. Pour beef broth, right from the can, over the cubes. Garnish with a slice or wedge of lemon or lime. NOTE: For variety add a fleck of spice to the beef broth before pouring over ice cubes, perhaps curry, nutmeg, cinnamon, allspice, or ginger.

WHITE MOUNTAIN REFRESHER

1 can (10¾ ounces) condensed
  cream of potato soup
1 soup can milk
½ cup sour cream
¼ cup finely chopped cucumber

In saucepan, combine all ingredients. Heat; stir occasionally. Beat until smooth with blender; or use rotary beater or electric mixer and strain. Chill 6 hours or more. Thin to desired consistency. Serve in chilled bowls. Makes about 3 cups.

SHRIMP GLACÉ

1 can (10¾ ounces) condensed
  cream of celery soup
1 soup can water
1 cup diced cooked shrimp
1 cup chopped fresh spinach
½ teaspoon grated lemon rind

In saucepan, combine all ingredients. Heat; stir occasionally. Chill 6 hours or more. Serve in chilled bowls. Makes about 3½ cups.

Twentieth-century chef Louis Diat invented one of the most famous frosty soups, Vichyssoise, at the Ritz-Carlton in New York City—and what a success it was! Now you can try Vichyssoise in at least three quick versions, or add your own to this chapter of cold summer soups.

VICHYSSOISE

1 can (10¾ ounces) condensed
cream of potato soup
1 soup can milk
Chopped chives or parsley

In saucepan, combine soup and milk. Heat; stir occasionally. Beat until smooth with blender; or use rotary beater or electric mixer and strain. Chill 4 hours or more. Thin to desired consistency. Serve in chilled bowls. Garnish with chives or parsley. Makes about 2½ cups.

VICHYSSOISE FLORENTINE

1 can (10¾ ounces) condensed
cream of potato soup
1 soup can milk
¼ cup cooked chopped spinach
Nutmeg

In saucepan, combine all ingredients except nutmeg. Heat; stir occasionally. Beat until smooth with blender; or use rotary beater or electric mixer and strain. Chill 4 hours or more. Thin to desired consistency. Serve in chilled bowls. Garnish with nutmeg. Makes about 2½ cups.

PINK VICHYSSOISE

1 can (10¾ ounces) condensed
cream of potato soup
¾ cup milk
½ cup tomato juice
Dash garlic powder
¼ cup chopped green pepper

In saucepan, combine soup, milk, tomato juice, and garlic. Heat; stir occasionally. Beat until smooth with blender; or use rotary beater or electric mixer and strain. Chill 4 hours or more. Thin to desired consistency. Add green pepper. Serve in chilled bowls. Makes about 2½ cups.

Dress-Up Garnishes

"Only the pure in heart can make a good soup" Beethoven wrote. The artistic can dress it up, he might have added. When soup comes to the table—hot or cold, thick or clear—a bit of contrast in texture, color, or flavor sets it off to appetizing advantage.

Achieve soup distinctiveness through garnishes such as these which are good on most any soup: chopped parsley, watercress, or chives—thin-sliced lemon or grated rind—sliced cooked mushrooms—sour cream or salted whipped cream—packaged stuffing—toasted nuts—sliced green onions—chopped ripe olives—crisp bacon—potato chips and corn chips—crisp cereal.

Many recipes follow for other ideas.

ZESTY PAN-TOASTED CRACKERS

1 **cup oyster crackers**
1 **tablespoon butter, melted**
Celery or onion salt

Add crackers to butter; heat. Shake pan to coat crackers with butter. Sprinkle with celery or onion salt. Especially good with tomato or chicken soup.

CHEESE CHOICE

Cheese adds a tangy accent to soups. Worth trying: shredded Swiss cheese on tomato rice soup. Grated Parmesan cheese on minestrone soup. Shredded sharp yellow cheese sprinkled on jellied consomme. Snippets (shapes cut from thin-sliced cheese) floated on top of soup (good on most kinds).

SOUR CREAM TOPPING

Try a dollop of sour cream atop soup—hot or cold. Good alone or combined with horseradish or watercress. Add parsley or chopped peeled cucumber for chilled cream of celery, chicken, mushroom soup or jellied consomme. Combine sour cream and chives to top beef broth, tomato, jellied consomme, or beef soup.

WHIPPED CREAM GARNISHES

Combine ¼ cup heavy cream (whipped) with ½ teaspoon prepared horseradish; spoon on green pea soup. Or to ¼ cup heavy cream (whipped) add 1 teaspoon grated lime rind, ½ teaspoon Sherry (optional) for jellied consomme. Or try ¼ teaspoon minced onion in cream for beef broth-tomato soup.

EASY DUMPLINGS

¼ cup packaged biscuit mix
4 teaspoons milk

Lightly blend biscuit mix and milk. Drop small amounts of dough from tip of a teaspoon into simmering chunky turkey or condensed vegetable beef soup. Cook for 5 minutes; cover and cook another 5 minutes.

VARIATIONS: 1. Season biscuit mix with 1 teaspoon minced parsley. Cook in chicken vegetable soup. 2. Add ¼ cup shredded sharp Cheddar cheese to biscuit mix; blend with milk. Cook in vegetarian vegetable soup. 3. Sprinkle dumplings with Parmesan cheese. Cook in minestrone soup. 4. Add 1 tablespoon chopped watercress or 1 teaspoon minced onion to biscuit mix; cook in turkey noodle soup.

CURRIED CRAX

⅛ teaspoon curry powder
1 tablespoon butter, melted
½ cup wheat squares or coarsely crumbled saltines

Stir curry powder into butter. Add crackers; heat to brown lightly. Stir often. TIP: Substitute ⅛ teaspoon leaf thyme for curry. Proceed as above. Good on most chicken soups or cream of potato soup.

ONION TIDBITS

¼ teaspoon instant minced onion
1 tablespoon butter, melted
½ cup cheese tidbits

Stir minced onion into butter. Add cheese tidbits; heat to brown lightly. Stir often. Serve on tomato or cream of chicken soup.

SOUP ACCENTS

Almond-Orange: Sprinkle chopped toasted almonds and grated orange rind on heated cream of asparagus or chicken soup.

Diced tomato: Float on jellied consomme.

Thin sliced onion: Float on top of shimmering jellied consommé.

Chopped celery: Sprinkle on consomme.

Chopped or thinly sliced pickle: Sprinkle on tomato rice soup.

Popcorn: Sprinkle on any soup.

Pretzels: Sprinkle on hearty or thick soups

CROUTON CREATIONS

Crisp croutons dress up soup easily, can be flavored "to your taste" quickly.

BASIC DIRECTIONS

1 slice white bread, cut into cubes
2 tablespoons butter or margarine, melted

In skillet, brown bread cubes in butter; stir constantly. Season to set off soup flavor.

BASIL OR OREGANO
Sprinkle croutons with ¼ teaspoon sweet basil or ground oregano. Serve with tomato or minestrone soup.

PARMESAN CHEESE
Sprinkle croutons with 1 tablespoon grated Parmesan cheese. Add to green pea or minestrone soup.

CURRY
Sprinkle croutons with curry powder. Add to chicken with rice or cream of chicken or green pea soup.

GARLIC
Melt butter in skillet; add ½ small clove garlic, minced. Lightly mix in bread cubes; cook over low heat, stirring constantly, until bread is crisp and brown. Serve on vegetable or green pea, beef or beef noodle soup.

SAGE OR THYME
Add dash of ground sage or leaf thyme to croutons. Serve with chicken with rice or vegetable soup.

Soups for All Seasons

FALL

Bring out the bikes! Brisk, clear days call for countryside pedaling. Picnic lunch includes vacuum of zesty soup. TEN-SPEED SIPPER: Combine 1 can each (10½ ounces) condensed beef broth and condensed tomato soup. Stir in 1½ soup cans water, 1 teaspoon lemon juice, dash ground cloves. Simmer a few minutes; pour into vacuum jug. Makes about 4 cups.

Color, color everywhere. A walk in the woods is a must. RUSSET SOUP greets your return home. Combine 1 can (19 ounces) chunky beef soup, 2 teaspoons ketchup, 1 teaspoon prepared mustard, and dash hot pepper sauce. Heat; stir occasionally. Makes about 2½ cups.

Geared for autumn gardeners: SEPTEMBER SOUP. Combine 1 can (10½ ounces) condensed onion soup, ½ soup can tomato juice, ½ soup can water. Heat; stir occasionally. Makes about 2½ cups.

Piles of crinkly leaves mean a job well-done. Reward weary leaf-rakers with HEARTY HAM GUMBO. Brown ¼ cup diced cooked ham in 1 tablespoon butter or margarine. Add 1 can (10¾ ounces) condensed chicken gumbo soup, 1 soup can water, and dash hot pepper sauce. Heat; stir occasionally. Makes about 2½ cups.

A diller, a dollar, a very hungry scholar loves hot soup at lunchtime. Dish up GOLDEN NUGGET BOWL soon. Combine 1 can (10¾ ounces) condensed turkey noodle soup, 1 soup can water, ¼ cup diced cooked carrots, and 1 tablespoon chopped parsley. Heat; stir occasionally. Makes about 2½ cups.

Football, glorious football! Cheer that team to victory with help from robust GRIDIRON WARMER. Combine 1 can (11¼ ounces) condensed green pea soup, 1 soup can water, and generous dash crushed thyme leaves. Heat; stir occasionally. Makes about 2½ cups.

Wood-chopper's dividends: CONFETTI CUP. Combine 1 can (10½ ounces) condensed chicken with rice soup, 1 soup can water, 1 tablespoon chopped parsley, and 1 tablespoon chopped pimiento. Heat; stir occasionally. Makes about 2½ cups.

Indian summer: Golden days, nippy nights. End leisurely twilight stroll with warming HARVEST MUG. Cook ¼ cup chopped green pepper, 2 tablespoons chopped onion with ⅛ teaspoon oregano leaves in 1 tablespoon butter or margarine until tender. Add 1 can (11 ounces) condensed tomato rice soup and 1 soup can water. Heat; stir occasionally. Makes about 2½ cups.

Going, going, gone . . . to a Saturday auction. Afterwards, gather friends and compare "finds" over bowls of CHICKEN CURRY SOUP. Brown ¼ cup slivered almonds and cook 2 tablespoons chopped onion with ½ teaspoon curry powder in 1 tablespoon butter or margarine until tender. Blend in 1 can (10¾ ounces) condensed cream of chicken soup, 1 can (10½ ounces) condensed chicken with rice soup, and 1½ soup cans water. Heat; stir occasionally. Makes about 4 cups.

Hurray for the old-fashioned hayride! For a fitting sequel, serve CARA-WAY BACON BOWL. Brown ½ cup ham cut in strips and cook 1 cup shredded cabbage and ¼ cup chopped onion in 2 tablespoons butter or margarine until tender. Add 1 can (10¾ ounces) condensed cream of celery soup, 1 soup can water, and ⅛ teaspoon caraway seed. Heat; stir occasionally. Makes about 3 cups.

Halloween whimsy: a pumpkin-carving party. Invite only friendly ghosts and offer them CASPER'S TUREEN. Blend 1 can each (10¾ ounces) condensed beef noodle, bean with bacon, cream of celery soup, 2 soup cans water, 2 tablespoons chopped parsley, and 1 tablespoon Worcestershire. Heat; stir occasionally. Makes about 6 cups.

Thanksgiving. Traditional turkey and trimmings? Then give your appetizer soup a twist. Serve GREEN PEPPER CREAM. In electric blender combine 1 can (10¾ ounces) condensed cream of celery soup, 1 soup can milk, ¼ cup chopped green pepper, and 1 tablespoon chopped onion. Beat at low speed until smooth. In saucepan, heat blended mixture; stir occasionally. Makes about 2½ cups.

Gobblin's good. Here's one yummy way to use that post-holiday turkey: PLYMOUTH ROCK SPECIAL. Cook 1 small onion, chopped in 2 table-spoons butter or margarine until tender. Add 1 can (10½ ounces) condensed chicken vegetable soup, 1 can (10¾ ounces) condensed turkey noodle soup, 2 soup cans water, 1 cup diced cooked turkey, and 1 tablespoon chopped parsley. Heat; stir occasionally. Makes about 6 cups.

WINTER

Under the misletoe: You'll kiss the cook who serves a customary oyster stew supper on Christmas Eve. Use condensed oyster stew and follow label directions. Garnish with slices of ripe olive or shreds of carrot or cheese. Finish the feast with apples, tangerines, Christmas cookies.

NEW YEAR'S BRUNCH PUNCH—hot and spicy. Combine 1 can (10¾ ounces) condensed tomato soup, 1 soup can milk, generous dash ground cinnamon, and dash ground cloves. Heat; stir occasionally. Garnish with whipped cream if desired. Makes about 2½ cups.

HAM TODAY, SOUP TOMORROW: Warm winter sports fans with soups that make the most of the last of your holiday ham.

1. OYSTER HAM STEW to brighten your "untrim-the-tree" party: Combine 1 can (10½ ounces) condensed oyster stew, 1 soup can milk, 1 cup cubed cooked potatoes, ½ cup diced cooked ham, 1 tablespoon chopped parsley, ⅛ teaspoon thyme leaves, crushed. Heat; stir occasionally. Makes about 3½ cups.

2. SPUNKY HAM BOWL to warm skaters from nose to toes. Brown ½ cup diced cooked ham with generous dash crushed rosemary leaves in 1 tablespoon butter or margarine. Add 1 can each (10¾ ounces) condensed cream of celery and chicken vegetable soup, 2 soup cans water, 1 tablespoon chopped parsley. Heat; stir occasionally. Makes about 5½ cups.

3. WESTERN NOODLE SOUP to pamper that snow-shoveling man. Brown ½ cup diced cooked ham and cook ¼ cup green pepper strips in 1 tablespoon butter or margarine until tender. Add 1 can (10¾ ounces) condensed chicken noodle soup and 1 soup can water. Heat; stir occasionally. Makes about 3 cups.

Time for storytelling by the crackling hearth, snug from Jack Frost's shenanigans. Pass the popcorn. Ladle the soup: ORIENTAL EXPRESS. Combine 1 can (10½ ounces) condensed beef broth, 1 soup can water, ½ cup thinly sliced carrots, ½ cup fresh green beans cut in 1" pieces, 2 teaspoons soy sauce, ¼ teaspoon sugar. Cover; simmer 15 minutes or until vegetables are tender. Stir occasionally. Makes about 3 cups.

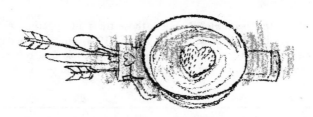

Crafty capers: You'll finish that patchwork quilt by noon. Wouldn't some-one else like to see it? Share some MOUNT VERNON GUMBO, too. Combine 1 can (10¾ ounces) condensed chicken gumbo soup, 1 soup can water, 1 cup frozen cleaned raw shrimp, generous dash hot pepper sauce. Bring to boil, reduce heat; simmer 5 minutes or until shrimp is done. Makes about 3 cups.

Love that KING OF HEARTS soup! Brown 1 can (about 2 ounces) mush-room stems and pieces, drained and cook 1 tablespoon chopped parsley in 1 tablespoon butter or margarine. Add 1 can (10¾ ounces) condensed chicken noodle soup, 1 soup can water, 1 tablespoon sherry. Heat; stir occasionally. Cut small hearts out of bread slices, brown lightly in butter. Top each serving with a heart crouton. Makes about 2½ cups.

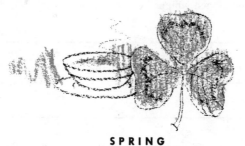

SPRING

Irish eyes are sure to smile when you celebrate St. Patrick's day with soup. Keep it simple. Just heat a can of cream of potato soup as directed. Garnish with parsley or watercress. Or you might serve green pea soup topped with a fluff of unsweetened whipped cream.

If April comes, can green be far behind? Forget the rain slickers and galoshes with PRIMAVERA POTAGE—one of the first signs of Spring. Cook ¼ cup chopped onion in 1 tablespoon butter or margarine until tender. Stir in 1 can (10¾ ounces) condensed cream of celery soup, 1 soup can milk, ½ cup drained cooked chopped spinach, dash crushed basil leaves. Heat; stir occasionally. Makes about 3½ cups.

Ten A.M. tennis twosome? By noon, those fresh air appetites will welcome GARDEN CHOWDER. Combine 1 can (10¾ ounces) condensed New England clam chowder, 1 soup can milk, ½ cup cooked carrots cut in strips, 2 tablespoons chopped parsley. Heat; stir occasionally. Makes about 2½ cups.

MORE MEATLESS MARVELS: A trio of hearty chowders. SHRIMP CHOWDER: Cook ¼ cup chopped onion in 2 tablespoons butter or margarine until tender. Blend in 2 cans (10¾ ounces each) condensed cream of celery or mushroom soup, 1 soup can each milk and water, 1 cup cooked shrimp (6-ounce can, drained), 2 tablespoons chopped parsley, dash pepper. Heat; stir occasionally. Garnish each serving with paprika. Makes about 3½ cups. TUNA CHOWDER: Substitute 1 cup drained and flaked tuna (7-ounce can) for shrimp. LOBSTER OR CRAB CHOWDER: Substitute 1 cup flaked cooked lobster or crab (6½-ounce can, drained) for shrimp.

Promise yourself an herb garden. Fresh thyme will accent dishes like elegant SPRING PEA SOUP. Blend 1 can (11¼ ounces) condensed green pea soup with 1 soup can water and ⅛ teaspoon ground thyme. Heat; stir occasionally. Garnish with unsweetened whipped cream or sour cream. Makes about 2½ cups.

Easter—and the soup should be easy. Whether the main course is ham or lamb, soups like chicken with rice and cream of asparagus make perfect preludes.

Remember Mom! Her Day merits a soup as pretty as a bouquet: MINTED PEA SOUP. Cook 2 tablespoons sliced green onion in 1 tablespoon butter or margarine. Add 1 can (11¼ ounces) condensed green pea soup; gradually blend in 1 soup can water. Add ½ cup sliced cooked carrots, 1 teaspoon dried mint leaves, crushed. Heat; stir occasionally. Garnish with sour cream. Makes about 3 cups.

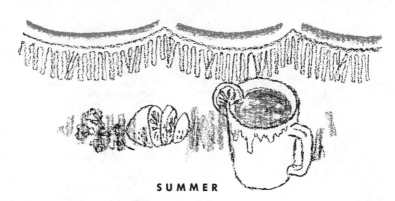

SUMMER

Hammock days. Let cool TOMATO TANG accent a lazy morning. Blend 1 can (10¾ ounces) condensed tomato soup and 1 soup can water. Stir in ½ teaspoon grated lemon rind. Chill 4 hours or more. Serve in chilled bowls; garnish with parsley or lemon slices. Makes about 2½ cups.

Wanderlust is alive and well in the campgrounds of America. So is snacking. Here's a campfire warmer: CONSOMMÉ RISOTTO. Combine 1 can (10½ ounces) condensed consommé, 1 soup can water, and ¼ cup cooked rice. Heat; stir occasionally. Makes about 2½ cups.

July 4th—fun, feasting, fireworks. Needed: Evening pick-me-up. YANKEE DOODLE DANDY. Cook ¼ cup chopped green pepper and 1 tablespoon thinly sliced green onion in 2 tablespoons butter or margarine until tender. Add 2 cans (10½ ounces each) condensed consommé, 1½ soup cans water, and 2 whole cloves. Simmer a few minutes to blend flavors. Remove cloves before serving. Makes about 4 cups.

As high as an elephant's eye—succulent August corn. Try some in CORN OYSTER STEW. Cook 2 tablespoons small green pepper strips and 2 tablespoons chopped green onion in 1 tablespoon butter or margarine until tender. Add 1 can (10½ ounces) condensed oyster stew, 1 soup can milk, and ½ cup cooked whole kernel corn. Heat; stir occasionally. Makes about 3 cups.

Sailing, sailing. Smallfries' delight: Spread 2 round crackers with peanut butter. Cut 1 saltine in half diagonally making two triangles. Stand the half cracker in the peanut butter to make a "sail." Float sailboat on soup. 2 sailboats for fair weather ahead.

Index

Notes

Notes

*"To make the best,
begin with the best—
then cook with extra care."*